"Phil A. Neel reports from far-flung pla[ces] do: a train full of migrant workers in s[ome] Cell, USA. Neel writes in a visceral and s[...] he everywhere finds, and he applies to [...] encounters a most unusual rigor. *Hinterland* is the geography lesson I've been looking for all year."
—Rachel Kushner, *Bookforum*

"Simply bracing . . . Neel makes the unifying, underlying dynamics hard to deny—dynamics of dwindling state resources, growing demands stemming from unfolding climate catastrophe and rising superfluity, and deepening threats to government capacity and legitimacy. This is stark terrain that too few scholars glimpse with any clarity. Its implications are massive."
—*Los Angeles Review of Books*

"Neel draws attention to the geography of class in Hinterland, identifying both a new working class and the global forces that have shaped it . . . Neel doesn't propose to solve any current 'What's up in Trump country?' debates. Instead he sets out to show the transformation, and often enough the hollowing out, of large tracts of twentieth-century life as the product of global capitalism . . . [Neel's book] honors the view from below or from the hinterland, where class is something that happens to you, like the weather but worse and more unrelenting. This emphasis has much to recommend it: ethically in its attention to lived experience, politically in its emphasis on concrete conflicts, intellectually in its alertness to variation and nuance . . . A meditation on the opacity of class experience, to those who live in it but also to those who theorize it." —*New Republic*

"Hinterland is where the future slouches toward Bethlehem. Phil Neel's dazzling journeys through the burned-over landscapes of end-time capitalism . . . compel us to rethink what class conflict looks like."
—Steve Fraser, author of *The Age of Acquiescence: The Life and Death of American Resistance to Organized Wealth and Power*

"Imagine Patrick Leigh Fermor and Karl Marx on a road trip through the hubs and corridors, empty rural tracts and dreary outer suburbs of rust-belt America in search of a central authority to whom one could lodge a complaint, and find no-one home—in fact, home itself gone . . . Ambitious, polemical, brilliant."
—Arlie Hochschild, author of the *New York Times* best-seller *Strangers in Their Own Land: Anger and Mourning on the American Right*

FIELD NOTES

SERIES EDITOR: Paul Mattick

A series of books providing in-depth analyses of today's global turmoil as it unfolds. Each book focuses on an important feature of our present-day economic, political and cultural condition, addressing local and international issues. Field Notes examines the many dimensions of today's social predicament and provides a radical, politically and critically engaged voice to global debates.

Published in association with the *Brooklyn Rail*

Titles in the series:

A Happy Future is a Thing of the Past: The Greek Crisis and Other Disasters
PAVLOS ROUFOS

Hinterland: America's New Landscape of Class and Conflict
PHIL A. NEEL

No Home for You Here: A Memoir of Class and Culture
ADAM THERON-LEE RENSCH

Smart Machines and Service Work: Automation in an Age of Stagnation
JASON E. SMITH

States of Incarceration: Rebellion, Reform, and America's Punishment System
JARROD SHANAHAN AND ZHANDARKA KURTI

HINTERLAND

*America's New Landscape
of Class and Conflict*

PHIL A. NEEL

REAKTION BOOKS

Published by Reaktion Books Ltd
Unit 32, Waterside
44–48 Wharf Road
London N1 7UX, UK
www.reaktionbooks.co.uk

First published 2018, reprinted 2019
First paperback edition published 2020, reprinted 2022

Printed and bound in Great Britain by TJ Books Ltd, Padstow, Cornwall

A catalogue record for this book is available from the British Library

ISBN 978 1 78914 213 6

Contents

Introduction: The Cult of the City

The train hurled through the hot, mist-damp blackness of southern China. If you stood in the barren cavities between cars, you could feel the air as it was sucked into the compartment via thin windows slit in the metal like narrow wounds. The stink of factories and endless, fertilizer-soaked fields pushed against the claustrophobic smell of food and bodies. Nothing was visible outside save for the few platforms we stopped at, small oases of yellow-lit concrete lodged within a jungle of limestone cliffs, cash crops and half-abandoned industrial sites all sinking in the hot darkness, a dull orange glow on the horizon like fires burning somewhere behind the karst plateaus. At each platform, more people entered, mostly migrant workers hauling their belongings on their backs in gigantic plastic fiber *mingong* bags, all the same pastel plaid. For the first eight hours, no one seemed to disembark.

Like me, none of the migrants had bought seats. Chinese trains have an elaborate hierarchy of ticket types, the lowest and cheapest being these standing tickets, which entitle you to entry but nothing else. Most people with these tickets stand or sit in the aisles and in the spaces between cars. If you're lucky, the other tickets were underbooked and you get a seat without the extra cost. Otherwise you can negotiate for half a seat shared with a stranger or simply squat in the mire of trash and sleeping bodies strewn down the aisle. Some people had come prepared with small, fold-out stools. Others sipped instant noodles as they slumped against their plaid plastic bags filled with whatever necessities they'd used to build makeshift lives in the dormitories and run-down rentals of some boomtown.

This was in 2012, during the tail end of the Chinese commodity bubble driven by the post-crisis stimulus package, much of which was funneled into large-scale infrastructure projects attempting to lay the groundwork for further development in the interior. As growth stagnated in the coastal capitals, boomtowns proliferated in lesser-known secondary and tertiary cities in the poorer provinces. But as the stimulus hemorrhaged and these interior hubs failed to grow at the same rate as their coastal forebears, the construction projects were finished with only a small measure of factory jobs left in their wake. As investment slowed, the migrants packed up their plaid sacks and moved elsewhere.

I stared out the slits in the metal into endless horizons of receding light. People shuffled up and down the cars, each looking as if they were searching for something specific, as if they'd lost someone they knew or heard of open seats in the next car over. But really they were wandering aimlessly. There was no one to find, and nowhere better that could be reached from here. Some would stop near me, red-faced, taking swigs from dark bottles of *erguotou*, a dizzyingly strong liquor distilled from sorghum. They'd offer me some and try to ask questions in English: where I was from, why I was here, what America was like. America is pretty much like China, I would tell them. No, they'd shake their heads. America must be better, they said, because in America you have guns.

Constellations

The stops became more and more infrequent, oases of concrete drying up as we approached China's far hinterland of emptied villages and hissing insects. In these areas, the vast majority of the working-age population has simply left, returning only during the Spring Festival, if at all. Five or ten years ago the villages would have been all old people and children, but today even the extended families tend to migrate if they can. Handfuls of elderly residents are all that remain, wandering through largely uninhabited villages encircled by the tombs of ancient ancestors. The train now felt like a bullet shot between two points. Its claustrophobic pressure was simply the physical force of our acceleration through the economy's outer atmosphere, compressing us within the steel carcass while the world itself was reduced to a series of points.

This isn't something unique to China, though the gigantism of Chinese development here, as elsewhere, provides a pristine example of the central tendency. The planet created by global capitalism is a serrated one. Some geomorphologists have taken to calling this economic earth the "technosphere," a skein of human-enhanced advection processes comparable in scale to those of the hydrosphere or biosphere, but marked by its intense tendency toward agglomeration and long-distance mass transport.[1]

Economic activity shapes itself into sharper and sharper peaks, centered on palatial urban cores which then splay out into megacities. These hubs are themselves encircled by megaregions, which descend like slowly sloping foothills from the economic summit before the final plummet into windswept wastelands of farm, desert, grassland, and jungle—that farthest hinterland like a vast sunken continent that met its ruin in some ancient cataclysm, populated now with broken-looking people sifting through the rubble of economies stillborn or long dead.

The Chinese megacity is different only in scale. If anything, decades of suppressed migration, agricultural protections, and strong property endowments in the countryside have made China less urban than it otherwise would be, despite popular images of traffic-clogged highways barely visible through dull red smog. Its official urban population sat at a mere 56 percent in 2015, with many smaller towns and sprawling village networks not quite cohering into true cities.[2] Compared to Japan, Europe, or the u.s., this is a meager number. But it is largely consistent with the global average of 54 percent (as of 2014), with the developed countries balanced out by the heavily rural parts of Asia and Africa. In recent years this share has only accelerated its increase, as smaller urban zones and megacities of 10 million or more all continue to grow—a rate that is fastest in the regions that have retained the largest shares of rural population.[3]

In a supposedly "post-industrial" economy, it is the dense metropolitan cores of "global cities" such as London, New York, Tokyo, and Shanghai that seemingly helm the world.[4] Overall, cities accounted for 90 percent of total economic output in the United States in 2011, with New York's urban area alone producing a Gross Metropolitan Product the size of Canada's entire GDP.[5] Concentration is particularly strong among high-end services, such as the FIRE (Finance, Insurance, and Real Estate) industries, producer services (like law firms or marketing agencies), and the slew of high-tech and professional positions staffed by the "creative class."[6] This produces a "great divergence," in which the population becomes increasingly segregated across cities and regions, signaled by trends in everything from voter participation to income and life expectancy.[7] Cities farther down the chain compete to reinvent themselves as international metropoles in their own right, attractive to both the high-tech, high-finance crowd and the sensibilities of the new hipster urbanists. Local governments pay premium fees to hire quasi-mystical consultants promising to reveal the rituals capable of attracting "creatives," whose exotic millennial culture seems somehow so far beyond the ken of the polo-wearing city administrator. Meanwhile, slums are demolished to make way for "walkable" neighborhoods peppered with cafés, CrossFit gyms, and cupcake shops. All of this is undertaken with a maddening zeal for the urban project itself, whether propagated by blind

faith economists or the bearded settlers of Brooklyn. And
such zeal has led to a situation in which the very core of urban
space—downtown and its flanking neighborhoods—has become
the blindingly singular focus of politics.

Crowds

But sometimes the seemingly determined arc of development
suddenly mutates. Crowds fill spaces built for capital. Tear gas
drifts through the financial district like the specter of finance
itself, as if that abstract swarm of shares, bonds, and derivatives
had achieved its own ascension, tearing free from prisons of
paper and computer circuitry like mist rising from a corpse.
Against this haunting shape, the crowds surge with their own
spectral sentience. At its most extreme, the very bedrock of the
city appears fissured, the plaza or square now the central fault
in a new urban tectonics. In the first sequence of uprisings,
the landscape seemed almost to become the subject of the
insurrection itself—the people of Egypt were condensed into
the roiling bodies of Tahrir Square, a mundane protest against
the demolition of Istanbul's Gezi Park was baptized in tear gas
and batons, and then born again in a million-body flood. In the
middle of winter in Ukraine, central Kiev was transformed into
a pyramid of flame. People wandered through the smoke and
snow beneath the pyre, their legs sunken in the gray wreckage.
The barricades were all slowly caked with ash, as if a new skin
had grown over everything, bodies surging like the muscle
underneath.

To those looking down from boardrooms and brownstones,
the new sentience gestating in the square can only appear
monstrous. Anyone who has been in such a crowd can feel
the power there, the strange new logics that emerge when
so many bodies are pushed together against the police and
the absolutely terrifying multiplication of violence made possible

in such moments. Those who seek to preserve the present order unleash their own demons against this new power, and at last the antagonism at the heart of that vast hostage situation called "the economy" descends into physical form as hooded youths hurl bricks against swarms of rubber bullets, the newly reborn god of the rabble wrestling with the old gods of capital.

Each insurrection of the early 2010s had a local impact proportionate to its ability to draw in residents of the non-urban or peri-urban hinterland (the slums, the *banlieues*, the council housing or even—as in the case of Bangkok in 2010—the impoverished countryside) and to fuse these populations, via shared action, with various fractions of the urban dispossessed, ranging from homeless people to graduates with no future. When such a combination was successful, the form it took effectively brought the city itself to the brink of death. The normal flows of goods, people, and capital all froze, as if such cities were in a state of paralysis—a condition military theorists coined "urbicide" after the sieges of Vukovar and Sarajevo during the Balkan Wars. For the liberal urbanist, this paralysis can appear only as the death of politics, since politics is for them simply a more participatory version of city administration taking place within the sphere of civil society. A central thesis of this book, however, is that urbicide as the product of insurrection is the point at which those excluded from the urban core and thrown out into that hinterland beyond suddenly flood back into it— this leads to the overloading of the city's metabolism, the death of urban administration, the local collapse of civil society, and therefore the beginning of politics proper.

The wealthy Syrian looking down from the high-rises of Damascus at the street protests of 2011 might in all likelihood have simply thought, who are these people? The answer, of course, was that many were residents of the country's own agricultural hinterland, made into internal refugees by severe drought and subsequent environmental and economic collapse. Others were residents of the city who simply saw no future in the city as it was. The feeling was much the same when urban liberals in America's coastal cities looked at the blood-red election map in November of 2016: their only possible response, who are these people? What is this place? The answer? This is the Hinterland. It is the sunken continent that stretches between the constellation of spectacular cities, the growing desert beyond the palace walls. These are the people who live there.

Separation

Looking from the city outward, the populations drawn from such places appear hyper-distinct and completely unrelated, each excluded in its own unique way and for unique reasons. The migrant, the refugee, the slum-dweller—all bring a subset of "issues" that are to be solved, if at all, by administrative organs, possibly stimulated from time to time by movements that "raise awareness." Only via this process can such populations come to be included in the "urban subject," and only on the condition that they themselves are incorporated into the fabric of the city itself. But beyond the city, where there is little question of inclusion, it becomes clear that these populations are also unified by something else: the commonality that comes from being increasingly surplus to the economy, though also paradoxically integral to it. This is the experience of class in the Marxist sense—the proletariat as the population that is dispossessed of any means of subsistence other than what is afforded by selling time for wages, simultaneously forced from the production process by technological development and nonetheless necessary to it, as its basic constituent.

And class cannot be understood without crisis. The global economic restructuring that has accompanied the long, slow crisis of the past several decades is often understood in purely sectoral or, at best, national terms. By sector, the economies of both the developed and developing world have undergone a tectonic shift, transferring their employment base onto high-tech production (infotech, biotech, aeronautics, and so on) and service industries, with profitability following suit. This is described in terms of "value added," as elaborate mythologies are narrated to explain the marginal values generated *ex nihilo* by the "creative" class, mirrored of course by the mass leveraging of debt across the FIRE sector, where arcane securities and impenetrable algorithms perform their monetary alchemy. Similarly, by nation, "globalization" has re-tiered the world, with each country developing through a sequence of steps on the ladder of production, all of which are synchronized via the world market.

These terms, by which both stalwart proponents and populist opponents understand the present economic order, are deceptive. While it is true, for example, that the expanding tertiary sector has been the primary area of job growth and profitability since the advent of the long crisis, this expansion has taken place along-side the ongoing stagnation of GDP growth itself, accompanied by secular increases in un- and under-employment and general precarity among workers. The historian Aaron Benanav details the trend for high-income countries:

> GDP per capita growth rates for those countries fell from 4.3 percent per year, on average, in the 1960s to 2.8 percent in the 70s, 2.3 percent in the 80s, 1.8 percent in the 90s, and 1.2 percent in the 2000s.[8]

Meanwhile, the periods of growth following ever-deepening recessions have tended to be "jobless recoveries," in which the gap between restored growth rates and restored levels of employment has widened with each crisis. During recessions in the early 1980s and '90s, employment recovered in a little more than two years. The most recent "recovery" took more than six.[9]

And Benanav's conclusions are not cherry-picked outliers. A similar case is made by the economist Robert J. Gordon based on a rigorous review of u.s. economic statistics dating back to 1870. Gordon's conclusion for the u.s. economy is simple: "economic growth witnessed a singular interval of rapid growth that will not be repeated."[10] For the u.s., this was the "special century" of 1870 to 1970, with the largest burst seen in the era of depression and world war between 1920 and 1970, when the growth rate was triple what it was in the periods before and after.[11] Though these dates are centered on u.s. growth trends, Gordon notes that other countries tend to follow a similar pattern, as early developmental bursts centered on a key nexus of "great inventions" slowly fizzle out into the new normal of slow productivity growth, albeit one disguised by the flashy success of the tech industry—which ultimately returns only meager upticks in the growth rate when compared to early industrial advances.[12] His conclusion for the immediate future is just as grim as Benanav's: "this book ends by doubting that the standard of living of today's youths will double that of their parents, unlike the standard of living of each previous generation of Americans back to the late nineteenth century."[13]

All of these trends, of course, are unevenly distributed. Gordon notes their uneven distribution according to generation, but geography is equally important. While some areas have been sheltered from the long global slowdown, others have slowly emptied out. The apocalyptic landscape of Rust Belt cities such as Detroit is likely familiar, but the phenomenon is not unique to the u.s., eu, or other developed nations. Deindustrialization is a general phenomenon. Despite its status as the "world's factory," for example, massive rust belts have formed even in China. Some are left over from the wave of deindustrialization that took place at the turn of the century, but many are the result of the recent, post-'08 wave of factory closures. Many of the migrant workers crowding into the train alongside me had once worked in production hubs such as the Pearl River Delta, only to be left without work as the factories closed in the early months of the crisis. Now, in China's west, they rode from one stimulus-fed boomtown to the next. As it does anywhere else, the crisis manifests differently city by city and region by region. In Guangzhou, old factory districts are refurbished into cafés and art galleries. In neighboring Dongguan, the population has simply hemorrhaged and empty factories are left to be reclaimed by the jungle.[14]

While deindustrialization is general, it has not led to a large-scale de-urbanization. During the many crises that have punctuated capitalist history, one common "solution" has been the expulsion of surplus population back to rural areas or outward to frontiers or foreign colonies. But the last half-century has seen capital run up against the geographic limits of colonial expansion at the same time that "returning to the land" was made essentially impossible in an increasingly urbanized world.[15] Instead of expelling workers, then, capital is forced to be more and more mobile, jumping to new frontiers of accumulation even while it cloisters itself from growing zones of unrest and unprofitability. This results in a selective concentration of capital within the urban fabric itself. While inequality between countries has decreased with global development, the inequality within countries has continued to skyrocket.[16] This is visible in the seemingly contradictory coincidence of opposing trends: as cities in the U.S. appear to be undergoing an economic and social renaissance, the number of U.S. families living under the World Bank's *global* poverty line ($2 per person, per day) more than doubled since the mid-1990s, reaching 1.5 million households in 2011.[17] Sometimes whole cities are abandoned, including their downtown cores, as a former industrial hub is transformed into a hollow node in the decaying Rust Belt. These become "traditional" inner-city slums in the American sense. But, more often, certain cores and corridors are preserved as hubs for "creatives" and global financiers while the rest of the city—particularly its not fully urban areas—are left to stagnate.

Meanwhile, rural regions are simply abandoned, becoming wastelands for global production. At best, they can hope to be transformed into recreation zones, military and prison complexes, or massive sites for primary production—swaths of countryside converted to mines, oil fields, or farms, or simply flooded to make way for reservoirs and hydropower projects serving the cities. Though sometimes geographically distant, most non-urban areas function as subsidiary zones for global capital and for the particular cities that happen to be closest to them—they are by no means outside the economy, and they therefore no longer constitute "peripheries" that are not yet fully subsumed into world capitalism. The global destruction of the peasantry has converted the periphery into a worldwide economic hinterland, defined by expulsion and exclusion. The hinterland, therefore, is not exclusively rural and is not characterized by the peasant politics of previous centuries. Where a "peasant" politics has survived, it has had to deal with fundamentally changed conditions of existence.

In this book, I define the hinterland largely by geography. It is a factor of distance from the booming cores of the supposedly "post-industrial" economy. "Deindustrialized" is not really equivalent to "post-industrial," however, and the hinterland is often a heavily industrial space—a space for factory farms, for massive logistics complexes, for power generation, and for the extraction of resources from forests, deserts, and seas. It is not an exclusively "rural" space, and it is by no means truly secondary to global production. Instead, it often acts as a disavowed, distributed core, distinct from the array of services and FIRE industries of the central city but more integral to the "immediate process of production," in which labor meets capital and value is produced.

But not all parts of the hinterland are as integral as others. I divide this book between a "far" and "near" hinterland, each of which contains its own distinct political dynamics. The far hinterland is more traditionally "rural," though now the "rural" is largely a space for disaster industries, government aid, and large-scale industrial extraction, production, and initial processing of primary products. Much of the far hinterland is also dominated by the informal economy, including black markets, the mass production of illegal drugs or other contraband commodities, and human trafficking—all of which is often synchronized with the formal economy. Though largely rural, the far hinterland also includes large urban zones of collapse, which exhibit almost identical characteristics. These include the remaining inner cities of the Rust Belt, many of which are seeing housing demolished at a rate that actually reproduces a quasi-rural landscape, as fields open where public housing complexes once sat. Much has already been written on the decaying inner city, however, and I therefore do not explore the topic here. I will begin, instead, with the rise of a resurgent far right in rural and exurban America, explored in Chapter One, before moving on to the economic background of this resurgence, analyzed in Chapter Two.

The "near" hinterland, by contrast, encompasses the foothills descending from the summit of the megacity. It is largely "suburban" in character, though this is something of a misnomer given the term's connotation of middle-class white prosperity. Much of the urban population in the u.s. (and in the world generally) lives in this near hinterland. In some countries, such as those in Europe, it takes the shape of towering apartment centers that ring the city, housing immigrants who staff large logistics complexes that exist beyond the urban core or who commute downtown to work in the service industry. Elsewhere, as in the cities of Africa and Latin America, the near hinterland takes the shape of the slum city, often walled off from wealthier exurbs and the downtown core. Due to its unique history of prosperous suburbia, the u.s. has its own distinct patterns, explored in Chapter Three, in which a "demographic inversion" in many cities has seen the transformation of old postwar suburbs into the primary settlement zones for new immigrants and for those leaving expensive urban cores. This inversion has generated new ghettos and new forms of resistance, epitomized by the suburban rioting in Ferguson, Missouri, in 2014. These political consequences are analyzed in Chapter Four, concluding the discussion.

Connections

After the first few hours on the train, a nearby migrant worker traveling with his wife and children offered me one of their fold-out stools. This was my first time in China, and I barely had a grasp on the language. He was a construction worker, he explained as much through hand signals as through broken English and half-understood Mandarin, but the cluster of brand-new apartment complexes he worked on had been completed, so he was headed back to his home village in Sichuan to visit family. Without vacation time, most migrant workers—just like low-end service workers in the u.s.—tend to use the space between jobs as a rough equivalent. After the visit, he would find work somewhere else in the country's west, maybe closer to home. Fumbling through my Chinese dictionary, I told him that I was from the country too. I grew up on a farm in the mountains, I explained, finding the characters for the animals that we raised and pointing to each as he helped me pronounce the tones.

Despite the inscrutability of the language and the vast distance between us, the similarities were equally salient. He was roughly my same height and weight, with dark hair similarly cut. We were the same age, and we had both worked a series of temporary or seasonal jobs, usually in manual labor. I asked what he wanted to do in the future, and he just held up his hands, as if to signal that any future he had left would only last for as long as they would. All around us there were other, older migrants, many missing fingers or nursing old wounds from the factory. I told him that I didn't know what I would do either. I tried to explain to him that I came to China because it was cheaper to fly to the western provinces, rent an apartment and enroll in Chinese classes than it would have been for me to go to university in the u.s. I worked as an English tutor for children. Many of my friends had left the u.s. too, fleeing student debt payments.

Though this book is about the distinctly American landscape of crisis and class, its conclusions are global in scope. The fundamental thesis is that the geographies detailed here are essentially international, since the crisis itself is a world crisis. New revolutionary horizons can emerge only via such connections, rather than via the ever-narrowing nexus of identitarian politics on offer in most activist circles, which share their political basis with the far right. Global deindustrialization has led to the collapse of the historical workers' movement and the communist horizon that attended it.[18] But this does not mean the death of class or the impossibility of a proletarian politics.

The things that unite us are precisely the things that keep us separate from everyone else. It's what the French ultra-left communist Jacques Camatte called "The Material Community of Capital." When the entirety of the world has been subsumed by capitalist production, the only connection we have with others is our increasing shared dependence on the obscure machinations of the economy. Rather than some ideal identity of blood or nation or shared urban life, we are really closest in the way that we are yoked together in our myriad separations of country, subculture, and employment tier. In such a situation, allegiances can be sorted only by one's level of antagonism towards this material community of separation, rather than one's position within it. I am united with the migrant worker by our shared class, age, and rural background —but in each the specifics differ so wildly that they seem to prevent any direct connection based on simple life experience. This is the unity of separation that is not yet the unity of any subjective orientation toward revolutionary potentials.

I tried to talk about riots in the u.s. and Europe, police murders, and the Arab Spring, and to ask about the riots and strikes common to Chinese factory cities—but too much was lost in translation. He just shrugged and pulled out his knock-off iPhone, pointing to a picture of a Rihanna album cover and signaling for me to put my ear near the speakers so I could hear the song. He liked the music but didn't know what she was saying, he explained. Could I translate? The train rocked back and forth, the tracks now curving up into the mountains of Yunnan province. Okay, I said, fumbling through my dictionary.

It was later now, and the lights in the cars had all been dimmed. I squinted at the pages, turned blue by the glow of the screen. A young, shirtless man with fierce eyes wandered past us aimlessly. It's a love song, I said. The construction worker nodded. We went around a sharp corner, and the shirtless man, not holding on to anything, tumbled into the pile of trash bags that had been accumulating between cars. Others squatted down to help pull him out, and he emerged with a bitter nonchalance, the same fierce look on his face. She's saying that she wants to set you on fire, I explained to the construction worker. The shirtless man wandered over to see what I was saying and others followed. So she doesn't have to burn alone, I continued.

Everyone nearby huddled around, not out of any particular interest but just because something seemed to be happening, fingerless workers gripping with what they could to stay in place, young women cradling cups of instant noodles as the train pitched back and forth, the steam rising out and weaving between bodies. She says that this is how you'll know where she's from, I said, translating literally and then wondering if maybe the metaphor isn't clear: the fire is how you'll know what she means, I try to explain. The iPhone screen glowed in the center of everything, coloring the steam from the noodles a soft electric blue. "Fire bomb," I again translate the term as literally as I can: *huodan*, an incorrect portmanteau which could as easily mean fireball or burning bullets, but with the tones wrong, it could also refer to a shipping manifest. In the eyes of the huddled people, the screen glinted back sharper than the original, compressed to blue sparks and blade-shapes cutting across dark pupils. Many had seen factory bosses beat and harass people like them; they'd seen civil police do sweeps in the major cities, arresting street hawkers and requisitioning their goods. But they'd also seen those same factory bosses walk out at the end of the day only to meet with mobs of migrants led by hometown associations—and those civil police outnumbered twenty to one by people no longer willing to put up with their abuse, the crowd chasing them into their police vans, overturning the vans, pulling the cops out limb by bloodied limb. The fierce glow was something more than a reflection. *Huodan*, I said again in garbled, mistranslated nonsense that nonetheless made sense. Fire bomb, burning bullets, a list of freight goods to be moved from one corner of the earth to another. The song ended and the screen of the phone went black but people still huddled together in the darkness.

one

Oaths of Blood

In northern Nevada, the soil alternates between a dull yellow and a jaundiced gray, intercut with the washed-out color of skin-rending sagebrush, a sweet-smelling corpse of a plant that clusters in vast broken archipelagos scattered across endless seas of hyper-flammable cheatgrass. When the sun is at its highest, creatures rest in the intricate root work of the brush, bodies entwined in the shade, where undead tendrils offer respite to predator and prey alike—small dens dug by families of wild foxes, crevices filled with shivering shrews, weasels, and mice; lightless sinkholes hiding legions of night-black beetles; roots entwined with rattlesnakes biding their time. Everything stinks of sun-heated sage, and after working a day on the range, you return to the trailer with the same smell, covered in thin layers of yellow-gray dust. That scent burns its way into your memory like a callus.

I was stationed in Winnemucca, a small mining-and-gambling town just east of the Black Rock Desert and south of the borders with Oregon and Idaho. The town is at the heart of a large swath of arid countryside, roughly equidistant between Bunkerville, Nevada, and Burns, Oregon, the two sites of the recent Bundy family standoffs that helped to spark the nation's resurgence of an armed and organized far right. Its economy resembles those of other rural counties in the far West, dominated by the boom and bust of global commodity markets, softened somewhat by seasonal work in tourism, wildland firefighting, and the management of federal land. I was there in 2011, still a boom year, with Chinese stimulus money driving up the price of natural resources and the economic crisis pushing gold prices to historic highs, all accompanied by the flow of new federal subsidies for natural gas pipelines and stimulus-funded employment programs.

It was also the first new boom for the growth of the far right. Having dwindled from their last peak in the 1990s, the election of Obama had stoked a nationwide resurgence of militias and affiliated groups, accompanied by massive purchases of arms and ammunition. Though nominally led by members of the old, more explicitly white supremacist militia movement (with its roots in posse comitatus, Christian Identity sects, and traditional neo-Nazi gangs), the new movement includes a number of young recruits who have no such history and who often hold no explicit white supremacist views. Many of these new recruits have been drawn from the generation of disaffected veterans who fought in the wars of the Bush era, only to return to hometowns crippled by economic depression and budget cuts. The movement has also been marked by a shift away from the militia as its sole basis for organizing, with numerous non-militia or quasi-militia groups forming alongside more traditional paramilitaries.

As part of the shift away from the militia, this rightwing resurgence has seen the emergence of new ethno-nationalist groups that have rejected traditional white nationalism in favor of a national anarchist or Third Positionist politics.[1] Instead of forming militias, such groups advocate the creation of cult-like "tribes" capable of building "autonomous zones" and returning to the land. These groups often use the language, tactics, and aesthetics of the radical left, and frequently exist within the same subcultures. Among the most prominent of these are clearinghouse organizations such as Attack the System as well as more organized groupings such as the Wolves of Vinland, a neo-pagan nationalist cult, organized like a biker gang and based around a land project they call "Ulfheim" near Lynchburg, Virginia, where the Wolves crowdfunded the construction of a traditional Viking longhouse.[2] The Wolves have three major chapters, with apparent organizational centers in Virginia, the Mountain States, and the Pacific Northwest, as well as a larger propaganda wing called "Operation Werewolf" which yokes together the participation of smaller groups nationwide. Much of their material is distinguished by a well-designed aesthetic, with clean logos plastered on professional-looking photos of muscle-strapped white men standing near fires, their faces painted with runes and shoulders covered by animal pelts, all accompanied by terse taglines well suited to distribution over social media.

Their work is popularized by semi-mainstream theorists like Jack Donovan, founder of the Wolves' "Cascadia" chapter and author of a series of books on tribalism and masculinity.[3] Donovan and the Wolves propose an across-the-board return to one's own "indigenous" roots, which will allow for the formation of a new confederacy of non-state, self-governing communitarian "tribes," defined in cultural terms but essentially reducible to ethnicities. They thereby discover a politics commensurate and compatible with the various ethno-nationalisms offered by the "decolonial" fraction of the miserable American left, and often understand themselves as part of this broader current. Such groups simply see themselves as building a place for white people within a communitarian confederacy of newly indigenous traditionalism, and their language often mirrors that of the left in arguing for a return to indigenous roots and the construction of autonomous zones.[4] Donovan, for example, often mixes left-wing and right-wing rhetoric in a single breath, arguing that the Wolves' back-to-the-land project in Virginia is

> about escaping to another world, not just for an hour or even a day, but for good. The Wolves of Vinland are becoming

barbarians. They're leaving behind attachments to the state, to enforced egalitarianism, to desperate commercialism, to this grotesque modern world of synthetic beauty and dead gods. They're building an autonomous zone, a community defined by face-to-face and fist-to-face connections where manliness and honor matter again.[5]

Similarly, Paul Waggener, one of the group's founders, clearly lays out the tribal basis of the organization: "When I say tribe, family, whatever, that's a very very well understood idea that these people are inside and those people are outside."[6] The tribe, then, is understood as a closed, communitarian space, opposed to both the state as such and any left-wing universalism.

The Wolves, though offering a pristine example of the far right's ability to craft an attractive aesthetic and mobilize in quasi-left political projects, remain a somewhat specialized fringe group within the larger right-wing resurgence. Similarly, the "Alt-Right," which rose to prominence with the election of Trump, has a media presence that far outweighs its significance —doubtless due to the fact that its particular brand of frat-boy fascism finds its base on college campuses populated by equally out-of-touch leftists, creating a virtuous circle of confrontations that spread widely on social media but largely draw from two very narrow demographics.

Once its figureheads were defeated—Milo Yiannopoulos via public outcry and Richard Spencer via repeated punches to the face—the phenomenon faded with the spectacle. By 2017, Spencer's "Unite the Right" rally in Charlottesville was widely recognized as an explicitly white nationalist event, its violent conclusion (with white supremacist James Fields plowing his car into counter-protesters, resulting in numerous injuries and the death of Heather Heyer) served only to further crumble the carefully cultivated image of the "Alt-Right," widening the divide between "patriot" groups and the more explicitly racist factions of the movement. Since the media backlash (and despite Trump's soft praise for the far-right protesters), even explicitly white supremacist organizations such as Vanguard America have rebranded themselves using the language and imagery of the Patriot Movement (see below), rather than the "Alt-Right," and Patriot symbols have begun to dominate the cultural field of conservatism in general. Though the "Alt-Right" phenomenon was significant insofar as it offered a space for a new far-right culture to gestate, it is only via the rise of new "Patriot" groups that this culture seems able to take flesh. At the same time, a certain degree of institutionalization came with the elevation of Steve Bannon into a central advisory position within the Trump administration. Though he has since exited the position, he has done so in the hopes of exerting even more influence via his ownership and management of various propaganda outlets. This represents an administrative mainstreaming of the far right, but doesn't signal much about its rank-and-file base.

Far more representative of the resurgence, then, are the original Patriot organizations such as the Oath Keepers and the Three Percenters, which have widespread bases of support (in the tens of thousands, measured by social media followings) and at least a few thousand actual members.[7] Both understand themselves as part of a vibrant "Patriot Movement" that is preparing for the coming of a second American Revolution, marked by civil war and social collapse, all inflected by a political philosophy in line with that promoted by Bannon, within and now beyond the Trump administration. Both include armed groups and regularly host paramilitary trainings, but neither group is simply a militia. Instead, they act as semi-decentralized umbrella organizations that include and exceed the activity of their constituent member groups, some of which are more or less traditionally organized militias and some of which are not. They often overlap (sometimes uneasily) with one another and with other far-right groups, but they have generally cut any lingering ties to explicitly white supremacist organizations and even tend to distance themselves from the more terroristic wings of anti-immigrant and Islamophobic movements in the u.s.—even while opposing the resettlement of Syrian refugees and using border patrols in Arizona for informal military training.[8]

The Oath Keepers portray themselves as an association of current and former military, police, and first responders opposing the totalitarian turn within the u.s. government. Their name comes from the notion that their members are simply staying true to the oaths they took to protect the American People—under present conditions, they argue, the protection of the People means opposition to the government and a refusal to carry out "unconstitutional" orders. Though it is still unclear how this anti-government politics will render itself under a Trump presidency, on a grander scale, they see resistance forming first in the far hinterland, where local residents can be organized into self-reliant militias and local governments can be won over to their cause to create a rural base of power, parallel and opposed to that of the federal government. These are the core unifying features of the group, though its individual wings often wrap these ideas up in a wide array of conspiracy theories, anti-immigrant rhetoric and veiled racism, the prevalence and precise character of which depends on the chapter in question.

The Three Percenters are a somewhat broader organization often overlapping with the Oath Keepers, and in recent years both have undergone a general, loose fusion. Their name is taken from the claim that only 3 percent of the u.s. population directly participated in the original American Revolution, and that, therefore, only a minority of individuals will be required to overthrow government tyranny in a second revolution to come. Emblazoned with the Roman numeral for three and a circle of thirteen stars representing the original American Colonies, the group's symbolism speaks to the commitment of its members to be this Three Percent when the time comes. Ideologically, both the Three Percenters and the Oath Keepers draw strongly though somewhat haphazardly from American Libertarianism, and both advocate attempts at local preparation and self-reliance. The Three Percenters, in contrast to the Oath Keepers, are a much more consistently and vocally anti-immigrant group, with much of their non-militia organizing efforts going into openly anti-immigrant or Islamophobic organizing, such as a series of marches aimed at preventing the resettlement of Syrian refugees in Idaho.[9]

In those early years in Winnemucca, these groups had only just begun to congeal. After our ten-hour shifts in the desert, my co-worker and I would relax with drinks and free games of pool at a local bar called The Mineshaft, a catchment for dead-eyed miners coming off a twelve-hour shift, Burners biding their time until this year's brief slice of drug-addled reprieve, vaguely white supremacist bikers looking for blood, broken-bodied cowboys and old Basque men trying to wait out the sun.[10] Smoke drifted between muffled shouts and pictures of topless women on motorcycles. On the weekends there were knife fights, fist fights, arguments, rounds of drinks, blood spilled in the dust outside. Sometimes train hoppers would wander in from the rail yard— mostly crust punk traveler kids with their dogs and denim jackets, soon chased off by the local sheriff who, rumor had it, used to rule the county with impunity, tying vagrants up and throwing them into the river. If I'd paid attention I would have maybe seen in all of this the slow encroachment of the new symbols over the old standards of bike gangs and run-of-the-mill desert Libertarianism. But at the time these things were just under the surface, swells forming before the wave took shape.

Wastelands

In the midst of a far-right movement dominated by Internet threats, spectacular street brawls and run-of-the-mill white male terrorism, the Patriot groups stand out owing to their focus on self-reliance initiatives. Faced with devastating declines in government services, many have stepped in to provide basic social services and natural disaster training. This is particularly notable in rural counties in states like Oregon, where the combination of long-term collapse in timber revenue and dwindling federal subsidies has all but emptied the coffers of local governments. In Josephine County, located in the Rogue River region of south-western Oregon, the sheriff's department is able to employ only a minuscule number of deputies (depending almost entirely on federal money), and often cannot offer emergency services after-hours. In 2013 the county jail was downsized and inmates were simply released en masse. In the rural areas outside Grants Pass (the county's largest city, with its own locally funded police department), the crime rate has skyrocketed, and the sheriff encouraged people at risk of things like domestic abuse simply to "consider relocating to an area with adequate law enforcement services."[11]

In this situation, the Oath Keepers began to offer basic "community preparedness" and "disaster response" courses, and encouraged the formation of community watches and full-blown militias as parallel government structures.[12] They offered preparation workshops for the earthquake predicted to hit the Pacific Northwest and "also volunteered for community service, painting houses, building a handicap playground and constructing wheelchair ramps for elderly or infirm residents."[13] While often winning the hearts and minds of local residents, these new power structures are by no means services necessarily structured to benefit those most at risk. The Patriot Movement surge in the county followed a widely publicized campaign to "defend" a local mining claim against the Bureau of Land Management (BLM) after the mine proprietors were found to be out of compliance with BLM standards. This sort of vigilante protection of small businesses, local extractive industries, and property holders (in particular ranchers) is often at the heart of Patriot activity.[14] And it is their skill at local organizing that makes the Patriots far more threatening than their more spectacular counterparts.

The Oath Keepers also piloted the Patriot Movement's "inside-outside" strategy within which local self-reliance initiatives were only one, slightly more direct, tactic among many. This strategy puts an equally strong emphasis on "inside" work via formal administrative channels (facilitated by entry into local government and the Republican Party) in a way that synthesizes well with the "outside" work they do in defunded timber country or along the u.s.–Mexican border, where they prepare and establish parallel structures of power. While filling in the holes left by underfunded law enforcement in Josephine County, for example, Patriot-affiliated politicians were also leading the opposition to new property tax measures that would have allowed the hiring of more deputies. This, of course, helps to widen the funding shortfall further, helping extra-state militias to step in and begin building their own power within the county.[15] The Patriot parties thereby seek to extend and secure the economic conditions for their own expansion.

The thing that makes the Patriots unique, then, is their recognition of the need to build power within these wastelands, and their surprising ability to outcompete the dwindling state and local progressives in this endeavor. These groups are essentially engaged in a battle for "competitive control," a term used by the Australian military strategist David Kilcullen (a senior adviser to General Petraeus in 2007 and 2008 and then special adviser on counter-insurgency to Condoleezza Rice) in describing the rise of guerrilla forces within the interstices of failing states. Kilcullen argues that the success of insurgencies such as the Taliban in Afghanistan as well as the rise of expansive criminal syndicates in places like Jamaica can both be explained by the ways in which such groups succeeded in providing "a predictable, consistent and wide-spectrum normative system of control"[16] that helps to win over a population buffeted by the chaotic inconsistency of economic and cultural collapse.

By providing material incentives that guarantee stability, combined with threats of coercion for those who oppose them, such groups become capable of making the population complicit in their rise, regardless of ideological positions. In fact, Kilcullen points out that in such situations (epitomized by all-out civil war), support for one faction or another simply does not follow ideology. People don't throw their weight behind those they agree with, and often many in a population can't be said to have any deep-seated ideological commitment in the first place. Instead, support follows strength, and ideology follows support. Political or religious attachment is often an after-the-fact development, preceded by the capable intervention of a pragmatic, functional partisan group that begins as a small minority of the population. The notion of the "Three Percent" is essentially the recognition of this fact, and the entire model of Patriot organizing follows the insurgent logic detailed by Kilcullen.

Deserts

In Nevada I could feel the Long Crisis with a terrifying intimacy, as if it was some sort of uncanny, bodily contact—like the feeling you get camped out in the swirling, galaxy-littered darkness of the open range when a reptile brushes up against your prostrate body. Except that the reptile at least shares with you some deep, serpentine connection, a lineage lost somewhere in the plummet of primeval time. The Crisis, on the other hand, is a vast creature, not contained by familiar scales of time or space. It is a social terror made of masses of machines and animals, yet not in any way kin to these components. And what we sense of it today is merely one of its many limbs extending backward from its true body writhing somewhere just out of sight, at home in our own incomprehensible future. In Winnemucca, the hotels were all sold out indefinitely because a natural gas pipeline was being built somewhere out there in the trackless waste, this one small capillary opened by the Crisis flooding the worthless dust with gold. Workers swarmed into every available space, drawn from all the poorest parts of the country, as well as the poorest parts of neighboring ones. Some of the old timers in the bar talked about this boom in the shape of booms long past, seamlessly mixing casual racism with moral derision for those slightly lower on the rungs of white trash than they. Those workers come in for two weeks—they'd say in quiet, even tones, the brims of their sun-cooked hats cutting into the smoke—and after two weeks they're buying tricked-out new trucks on credit, hauling those big families in.

Yet everything remained somehow just out of sight. I never saw the pipeline, though the workers flooded through the hotels and restaurants and casinos around me. Every morning buses filled with people departed from a lot near our trailer park, some heading to the pipeline, but most carrying workers out to distant mines. Shipments of gold and silver were trucked out of these mines periodically, surrounded by heavily armed paramilitary convoys. But the mines remained tucked far out of sight behind mountain ranges and layers of perimeter fencing. Meanwhile, my co-worker and I would drive out every morning far into the desert, where we removed fencing put up by an identical crew almost a decade ago. We could see distant ranches, mostly growing alfalfa with water drawn up from hidden aquifers, but we rarely saw another person.

Every couple weeks, our bank accounts were filled electronically by the Department of the Interior out of stimulus money allotted to the BLM during the bailouts. Everything seemed animated by an invisible force, all choreographed in some indecipherable ritual that simply was not meant for us. The sparse character of the desert seemed to draw the Crisis so much closer because it stripped away everything but this ritual, making peoples' orbits around the invisible gravity of capital discernible against the desert's flat plane. There was a sign just off the interstate near a small trailer-town called Golconda that had two arrows, one pointing north and one south. The first arrow said "Mines," the other "Ranches." We drove somewhere between the two to get out into the mountains, our orbits only small, errant arcs cast between occupations of greater gravity.

The Crisis is maybe most visible in the desert because the Crisis makes deserts. And it is these deserts that make the militias—or at least that make them an actual threat. The grim potential of these new Patriot parties arises via their ability to organize in the vacuum left by the collapse of local economies. It's easy for city-dwellers to dismiss the militias as simple far-right fanboys playing soldier in the Arizona desert, but that's because the real deserts are largely invisible from the metropolis—they are simply too far beyond its walls. The progressive narrative, embodied in an entire subgenre of think piece that we might simply call Tax Collector Journalism, therefore tends to treat these issues as if nearby ruralites just "oppose taxes" and therefore bring such funding shortfalls upon themselves. A slightly more sinister variant argues that, by backing candidates that reject increases in property tax, small, often out-of-county Patriot groups actually construct the crises facing these rural areas.

But these positions are nonsensical when we consider the fact that the collapse of revenues drawn from the land via extractive industries also means a declining property value for these lands and therefore a diminishing base of property taxes to draw from, all accompanying the disappearance of any commodity tax from timber sales, for example. To claim that this crisis was somehow "created" by anti-tax conservative ruralites or by small, relatively recently developed anti-government groups simply ignores that the basis of tax revenue is in industrial production, whether taxed at the level of capital, commodity sale, land ownership, or wage income. Less industrial output means either fewer taxes or a higher share of tax-to-income for most residents. Increased property taxes likely cannot be afforded by small landholders, for whom employment is sparse—and therefore the progressive's alternative of increasing property taxes is simply a program of dispossession for small landholders. It is no wonder, then, that these smallholders align themselves with ranchers, miners, and even larger corporate landowners (all of whom will be paying the largest lump sum in taxes) to oppose such measures.

It is here that the class basis of the far right begins to become visible. With new members joining the Patriot Movement drawn from a generation less convinced by the old militias' narratives of racial supremacy, the ideological focus of such groups has instead turned largely to issues of land politics. Visions of race war have been replaced by a (nonetheless racially coded) prophecy of oncoming civil war that pits diverse, liberal urban areas against the hinterland. It is easy to seize upon the more conspiratorial aspects of these fears (such as the claim that the UN is set to invade the U.S., with the help and preparation of the federal government) in order to dismiss these movements wholesale, but doing so tends to obscure the fact that these groups are responding, however incoherently, to their experience of the Long Crisis and the new geography being created by it. The results are inevitably grim and occasionally made visible in sweeping acts of political devastation, the urban liberal weeping at the shore of a blood-red ocean stretched between California and New York—an expanse somehow invisible until November 8, 2016, the 18th Brumaire of Donald Trump.

In reality, the far right's political base is not defined by sheer xenophobia and idiocy, and their political analysis, though sprinkled with occult themes and mystical logic, is not entirely hollow. To take a common example, the idea of George Soros secretly funding the most violent aspects of things like Occupy Wall Street and Black Lives Matter is a common trope, and it is only the more extreme version of a widespread perception that urban elites use forms of government patronage (in particular welfare and affirmative action) to buy the loyalty of minority groups and thereby turn them against "working people" who have no access to such patronage. Progressive critics often point out the ways in which this theory and many affiliate conspiracies mimic the anti-Semitic narratives of the old militia movement, drawn from the historic far right. But what this critique misses is the simple fact that these conspiracies approximately, if incorrectly, describe structures of power so pervasive as to be mundane to most people.

The Democratic Party does (obviously and publicly) fund "radical" projects as a method of co-optation (rather than radicalization, as the right would have it) in its constant cultivation of a strong, radical-in-garb-but-centrist-at-heart base among labor unions, NGOs, local governments, and any number of "community" organizations claiming to represent particular minority groups or simply "people of color" as a whole. This patronage is not evenly allotted to the urban poor, however, and it largely does not come in the form of "welfare" as the far right argues, but instead as grants, campaign funding, charitable donations, and services provided by churches, NGOs, or local governments—much of which is allotted to the upper-middle-class segments of disadvantaged populations, rather than those most in need. This method of co-optation and recruitment is therefore part of a real alliance built between the liberal upper segments of dispossessed urban populations and the particular fraction of elites who fund the Democratic Party. This is the Democratic Party machine. There is nothing conspiratorial about it.

The Carhartt Dynasty

The Republican Party operates on a roughly symmetrical base built up among rural white sub-elites and a whole array of urban or peri-urban petty-capitalist interests. Most of the Patriot groups essentially acknowledge this in their rejection of both parties, but groups like the Oath Keepers and Three Percenters recognize openings in the base of the Republican Party that do not exist for them in the base of the Democratic Party, due to the Republicans' extent into the very areas of rural devastation that Democrats tend to ignore. Their attempt at tactical infiltration of this base in order to widen the power vacuum in which they operate is then seen by urban progressives as more evidence that conservative Republicans are somehow secretly behind the economic devastation experienced in these areas—and if poor ruralites only had better information, they would vote for Democrats who would raise taxes and thereby fix the funding shortfall.

But, again, it all returns to the issue of shrinking industrial output leading to a shrinking tax base. It is not "taxes" as such that the population opposes here, but the twin dependencies wrought from the economic collapse: on one side, people in rural areas are increasingly dependent on federal funding for employment (in wildland firefighting, in forest management, in local school districts and healthcare systems almost entirely maintained by federal aid, in agricultural production sustained by subsidized government purchase programs), and on the other hand they therefore experience class exploitation as largely a matter of rents, rather than wages.[17] This leads to a populist analysis that emphasizes this form of exploitation and its attendant crises over all others, obscuring the deep interdependencies between what such populists portray as the "real" economy and the "false" economy of finance. It should not be surprising, then, that the far right has seized upon this and put issues of land management and local governmental authority at the forefront of its political program. The border patrol operations staffed by such militias are often treated as mere training grounds for near-term confrontations with the federal government in the American interior and long-term confrontations with opponents in the new civil war to come. The bulk of the popularity of the Patriot Movement has come not from such patrols, but instead out of direct confrontations with federal agents, all of which have ostensibly been protests about land use in the rural West.

The first of these was the Bundy ranch standoff in 2014, in Bunkerville, Nevada, followed by the slightly smaller Sugar Pine mine defense in Josephine County in 2015, and, finally, the occupation of the Malheur Wildlife Refuge in 2016, in Burns, Oregon. Despite being concentrated in a handful of states, the activities of this far western wing of the Patriot Movement have had a cohering effect on the far right at the national scale. There have thus far been no correlates among the militia movement of Michigan, or the KKK in Louisiana, though members of such groups certainly form part of the support base for the western Patriots. Similarly, the anti-immigrant border patrols in Arizona have been happening for over a decade now, and, though an important component of many far right groups' training, these patrols have failed to garner the same kind of widespread attention and popularity. This is because the specific land politics of the far western hinterland have offered the new right-wing movement an effective theater in which to oppose rent-taking and thereby form the rudiments of a mass base.

The crux of Patriot Movement land politics is the desire to see federally controlled lands returned to local management in order to revive long-dead local timber, mining, and ranching industries. At the same time, they argue that the devolution of federal power to states and counties will allow local communities to manage their own affairs. The harder edges of the movement (the "constitutional sheriffs") even argue that county sheriffs have a constitutionally mandated right to selectively apply laws passed at higher levels of government, and therefore sheriffs can act as a protective shield against state gun control laws, government surveillance, and the sort of federal mandatory-minimum charges applied to people like the Hammonds, whose long-term imprisonment for arson on federal land was the focus of the Malheur occupation. Though somewhat distant from the interests of poor whites in the eastern states, these political foci make perfect sense in the far West, where the bulk of the federal government's more than 630 acres (255 h) of land is located (mostly in eleven continental states plus Alaska).[18] In Nevada, the federal government owns nearly 85 percent of the state's land; in Oregon, the number is just over 50 percent; and in Idaho (the stronghold of the Three Percenters), it's around 60 percent.[19]

Much of the immediate conflict inspiring the confrontations that have magnetized the far right has been explicit conflicts over federal rents charged for land use by miners and ranchers. Different states have different levels and structures of management, but the bulk of this land is overseen by either the BLM (35.9 percent) or the Forest Service (32.8 percent).[20] Though both of these agencies are targeted by Patriot groups, the BLM's role in overseeing grazing and mining rights has been the root of all three major occupations in the West thus far. Though often blown out of proportion and incorporated into ideological claims that privatization as such is superior to any sort of government ownership, it's hard to argue with the fact that these federal agencies are often corrupt and certainly fall short of their original mandates.[21]

While working for the BLM, the head of our office used to brag that the agency brought in five dollars for every four tax dollars put into it, while the Forest Service brought in four for every five.[22] Similarly, stories of BLM corruption were rife even within the agency, with people whispering at marked-down land sales on the edge of Vegas during the housing bubble. Much of what the BLM does, in fact, is apply a vast and bureaucratic system of rents to those using the lands under its domain. This takes the form of fees charged for the recognition of mining claims (the cause of the Sugar Pine conflict) as well as grazing fees for cattle ranches (the direct cause of the Bundy Ranch standoff and the indirect cause of the Malheur occupation). As the direct interface between ruralites and the federal government, the BLM is a natural focus for the anti-rent, local-control politics of the Patriot Movement. But it also creates a real tension in these rural areas between those who subsist directly or indirectly off these rents and those who pay them (even while they may themselves benefit from similar purchase-end subsidies or government price-setting programs in the price of agricultural goods).

Much of the genuine opposition to the Malheur occupation, for example, came from the Burns area itself. According to data from the American Community Survey for the city of Burns (which does not include the surrounding county or the neighboring Burns Paiute Reservation),[23] government workers compose more than a third of the population (37.3 percent), and workers in agriculture, forestry, fishing, hunting, and mining are only half of this (17 percent). Meanwhile, local services such as retail make up only a little less (14.6 percent), but this is by definition dependent on the base industries that receive inputs from outside the area economy (that is, the government workers' wages—originating in tax money in excess of that produced in the region—and the ranchers' income, originating in exports of beef, both go to support the local grocery store). The divergence between the two largest categories is narrowed somewhat at the county level, with government workers at 30.3 percent of all employees; agriculture et al. at 27.2 percent; and retail only slightly diminished at 10.5 percent.[24] The image here is nonetheless one of a bifurcated employment structure, with a large chunk of the populace dependent on federal government inputs for their employment, and another large chunk dependent on government employees' wages for their jobs in the local economy. It is only natural, then, that something like the Malheur occupation would not necessarily win over a majority of the local populace, who not only do not oppose federal land management, but in fact depend on it for their livelihood. In Burns, the Patriots were ultimately outdone by the state in the game of competitive control, since the state itself provided enough stability to the population via its own normative framework, against which the Patriots could offer no real alternative, unlike in the more severely underfunded Josephine County.

Many urban critiques of the Patriot Movement have focused on these facts to construct "outsider" narratives of the Patriots, in which these militias enter local "communities" from elsewhere in order to sow disorder, against the wishes of the local population. Organizing against the militias is then portrayed as simply the upholding of the status quo via the silent majority, afraid to speak up when faced with the influx of heavily armed men. But these narratives tend to obscure or at least ignore in practice the actual conditions of economic collapse in the countryside, and simply reinforce the state's own position relative to rural areas in the far West, which is one of continued, contingent dependence and fierce competition for a shrinking pool of government jobs. The work of groups like the Portland-based Rural Organizing Project is a case in point. Urban liberals are paired with locals within the progressive establishment to build grassroots opposition to the militias, but when it actually comes to offering some sort of solution for the widespread economic problems of these areas, the focus is not on building local regimes of dual power to oppose the current economic system but instead to push for increased taxes and petition higher levels of government for more extensive payouts.

The experience in Burns also hints at the fact that many of those who are most adversely affected by government rents are not necessarily the poorest rural residents, or even average rural-ites. Such fees, combined with property taxes, disproportionately affect landowners and the proprietors of local extractive industries, as well as a wide variety of small businesses struggling to survive amid conditions of widespread economic collapse. The Bundys themselves are a striking image of the class of landholder that forms the figurative and financial backbone of the Patriot Movement: their land value, combined with their yearly income, actually puts them in the upper income brackets of such counties. Similarly, mine owners in southern Oregon or mill proprietors in Idaho are the literal holders of capital in their respective areas. They are a petty capitalist class that appears "working class" only through constant, active contrast with well-heeled coastal elites. An important part of this contrast is the fact that they do regularly work their holdings themselves (even while they oversee far less well-off, largely seasonal employees), and are substantially poorer than plenty of urban professionals, not to mention financial elites. Equally important is their constantly maintained, self-aware aesthetic, an amalgamation of traditionally middle-American clichés cultivated by large patriarchal families like the Bundys, variants of which are easily identifiable in most rural areas—the many local dynasties signified by their big trucks, camo hats, and Carhartt jackets, all often just a bit too clean and new.

It is this class fraction that is the real heart and focus of the Patriot movement. It is their property that is defended, and they are portrayed as the only forces capable of reviving the local economy. The devolution of federal lands to local control entails effective privatization of these lands into the hands of local holders of cattle and capital—those sleeping gods of the Old West, which the Patriots hope to awaken. All of the other participants in the Patriot Movement (many of whom are less-well-off veterans and other working-class locals) are nonetheless acting in accordance with the interests of the Carhartt Dynasty. There is little evidence that mass support for this politics extends all the way down, and much evidence that simply suggests that rural proletarians, similar to their urban counterparts, have been unable to cohere any substantial political program that has their interests at heart. In such a situation, we again see that support follows strength and belief trails far behind.

Blood Debt

I, my co-worker, and most of the other residents of the trailer park in which we lived, were driven in our invisible orbits across the gold-gray desert of northern Nevada by the twin gravities of wages and debts. My co-worker had wanted to get work on a fire crew, where the wages were better, but he had no experience and no family connection to any of the contractors. He was originally from Washington state, and his car broke down in Reno while he was looking for work. He was forced to settle for what he could find in the city, still hard-hit by the collapse of the housing bubble. In the end, he found a job going door-to-door selling vacuums. His part of the job was the exhibition, in which he came in and vacuumed people's floors for them before the other employee joined him and tried to sell them the vacuum on an installment plan. In order even to be paid minimum wage, however, he had to be allowed into a certain number of houses to exhibit the vacuums. In the end, he told me, he'd basically just go to people's doors and beg them to let him vacuum their floors so that the company would pay him.

This gave him enough cash to drive out to Winnemucca for the BLM job, which he hoped would help him pay off his debts. We often compared debts—one of the foundational rituals of the millennial generation (after selfies, of course). Mine were substantially fewer than his, almost exclusively from a $5,000 loan taken out to attend the last two years of college, which had quickly compounded until it was somewhere between $6,000 and $7,000. The monthly payments could not be deferred any longer, though they cost about as much as I'd been paying for rent in the trailer park. His debts were expansive, but not unusual for people our age. Part came from student loans—he'd been convinced by high school counselors to attend an expensive private school, where he learned how to read Egyptian hieroglyphics and dropped out before getting a degree. These summed above $10,000, before interest. Another portion came from medical bills. His family was poor and could not afford adequate insurance. He'd broken an arm once in a stupid accident (adding a few thousand) and also been hit in the head by an axe when the blade broke from the handle while chopping wood (adding several more thousand, with the necessity of hospital stays, brain scans, and all manner of painkillers). The head injury disqualified him from joining the Coast Guard, the one employment opportunity that actually seemed feasible and appealing, as he'd been a professional lifeguard and competitive swimmer. So, crippled by tens of thousands in debt, he made his way out into the desert, hoping that a fire would hit nearby and the crews would need extra hands.

As one of the poorest generations in recent history, debt and rent are the defining features of our lives. It is this fact that makes the current incarnation of the far right an actual threat, because it increases the probability that some variant of present-day Patriot politics might actually find a mass base, as a program formulated specifically to oppose the extraction of rents from an unwilling population in the far hinterland is translated into a more general opposition of rents as a primary form of exploitation in contemporary capitalism. This could rapidly move the far right inward, so to speak, building them a base among the poorer denizens of the sprawling American city, in the same way that both left- and right-leaning populist movements have found a base in an alliance of small proprietors, petty landholders, and the various members of the surplus population in Europe, Latin America, and Asia. The continued obliviousness of the urban liberal (most recently exhibited as a maddening overconfidence in a candidate as unpopular as Hillary Clinton) only helps the far right rise to power unopposed and largely invisible, its base in the exurb, the rust belt, or the third-order capitals of largely hinterland states like Idaho or Montana.

But can the far right offer any sort of solution to the Long Crisis? How can they represent the future when all

the demographic trends seem to be going against them—
urbanization, immigration, diversity, and even "littoralization,"
in which population becomes increasingly concentrated along
the coastlines? The truth is that, at present, the most vital Patriot
politics is largely limited to its current field of operations within
the far West, though it may be possible for new strongholds to
arise in Appalachia, the historic heartland of white poverty.
Smaller groups of weekend warrior militias will certainly pop
up elsewhere, and plenty of far-right violence is bound to emerge
in all the old breeding grounds of racial resentment, but there are
presently few places where collapse is so salient and the force of
the federal government offers itself so clearly as an enemy figure,
at least to the white population.

Though somewhat counterintuitive, the election of Donald
Trump will also likely have a dampening effect on the most
extreme wings of the far right, even while it emboldens a minority
to violent action. In part, this is because extra-state militias
affiliated with the far right tend to grow most strikingly under
Democratic presidents and to disperse under Republicans. When
a right-wing government is in power, federal agencies become a
more ambiguous force in the eyes of the far right. At the same time,
Trump's government is almost certain to absorb large numbers
of the far right into its own institutions. This is a terrifying
phenomenon, of course, but it will also likely drag much of the far
right back to center, at least for a while, since institutionalization
is in essence submission to the fraction of the elite bankrolling
those institutions. Meanwhile, the gutting of federal agencies and
the devolution of ownership (now an actual possibility) of some
federal lands to state and local governments may have contradictory effects. Rural areas will see further decline as federal funding
diminishes, and local control of land use is unlikely to restore
profitability in any substantial way. In essence, the election of
Trump represents a premature seizure of power, opening more
potentials for the far left than for right-wing militias.

A new American fascism will not spring fully formed from the body of the Oath Keepers or the Three Percenters, nor from some unholy alliance between these groups and their more traditionally racist counterparts farther east. The far right cannot be sustained if it remains sequestered in the far hinterland, which is, after all, increasingly depopulated. The focus given here to the Patriot Movement is instead due to its nearly systematic encapsulation of the kernel of far-right politics in the near future. With the abolition of rents, the Patriot Movement envisions a return to the "real economy" through the revival of extractive industries across the American West, accompanied by the extreme localization of political power. Aside from the magnetizing effect of the various Patriot standoffs in the far West, it is this populist ideology of the communitarian "real economy" that makes the Patriot Movement of the western states, alongside Third Positionist groups like the Wolves of Vinland, an image of the future far right in microcosm. After all, Trump's economic program, drawn from Bannon's philosophy, is almost identical, though writ at a much larger scale: raise tariffs, build walls, deport outsiders, and thereby begin the reconstruction of domestic industry, driven by the "real" economy of manufacturing and resource extraction. The main difference is simply one of scale, and whether the driving force of this economic revival will be large industrial corporations unified through a new national investment drive or instead the vital force of the "entrepreneur," petty proprietor, or even "tribe," unified by local autonomy.

Barbarians

Those debts driving us to and fro across the desert were only one part of a vast ritual forcing human life into endless, mechanical processes determined by the vastly irrational rationality of an economy that is premised on infinite growth. But the ritual is simultaneously one of expansion and of separation. Everything blooms outward and splinters apart. Each individual is gradually alienated from all others as the heart of production becomes more opaque, the connection between every node in the supply chain more distant, and the basic infrastructure of the world more complex. The ritual reaches down to the depths of human identity. We are defined increasingly by work and debts and purchases and each seems every year to resemble more the others until maybe sometime soon all three will simply fuse into a single form of near-complete evisceration. Our families grow smaller, our groups of friends diminish. Our subcultures are evacuated of all sacrifice and intimacy until they resemble little more than many minor bureaucracies propping up the great palace of consumption. When some fragment of the communal does find some space to congeal in the world's wastelands and factory floors—maybe in the midst of a riot, in the heat of a war, in the cold lonely life led in high steppes and deep mountain valleys not yet fully subsumed by crisis and capital—this fragment is ultimately found, pieced apart, drained of its intensity until it also can be thrown into that same dead, world-rending dance. The ritual has neither name nor mother tongue, but we communists call it the material community of capital.

Since this material community unifies only through a wide-ranging alienation that forces all individuals into dependence on its own impersonal infrastructure, the emergence of new, intensive communal practices are a recurring threat. All unity that is not the unity-in-separation offered by the mechanisms of the economy poses at least some level of risk, since such spaces offer the germinal potential of a dual, communal power capable of seizing and repurposing this infrastructure to truly human ends. Most of the time this risk is minimal, and communal structures are indeed created and preserved by market mechanisms in order to offer a false sense of respite, escape, or "tradition," each of which is strongly hemmed by the surrounding economy and almost always linked to it as an object of consumption (Burning

Man) or a source of credit (such as church- or clan-based lending associations). The ejection of growing segments of the population from the immediate sphere of production also ensures that the old threat of a global, communal archipelago arising from the "workers' movement" is not reproducible in the present moment.

This also means that what we might call "traditional" Fascism or Nazism is not coming back in any recognizable form, since these far-right phenomena were born of a now-extinct mass politics, their programs and aesthetics developed through a combination of mimesis and romantic rejection of the workers' parties of the twentieth century. The contemporary far right can only be characterized as "fascist" or "neo-fascist" insofar as one hollows these terms of their historical content, until they designate little more than the inclusion of racist or misogynistic elements in a political program. As a shorthand, "fascism" is accurate enough, but at the theoretical level it tends to imply a false historical analogy. The new far right is still embryonic. It's difficult to predict exactly how it will develop, but the conditions that determine this development are more or less visible.

One dimension of the intense fragmentation of the proletariat has been an increase in self-employment and petty proprietor-ship, fragments of the middle strata that have always become active elements in right-wing populist upsurges, and for whom the radical localization offered by national anarchists, Third Positionists, or Patriots seems to accord with common sense.[25] Another dimension is the fact that, without mass industrial production and the workers' movement that attended it, com-munal spaces are scarce and their absence felt more intensely. Rather than developing as a form of romantic communitarianism contra the scientific communism of the workers' parties, the far right today finds the most success in its capacity to intervene in the spectacular communal events opened in moments of insur-rection, as well as in its ability (especially after the insurrection) to outcompete the anarchists in their own game of local service provision. Faced with such strategic openings, the far right can mobilize its connections to police and military bureaucracies as well as the criminal and mercenary underworld in order to assemble and deploy its resources much faster than its largely undisciplined, untrained leftist opponents.[26] In this way, the militia or tribe is capable of fusing with enclosed national/ cultural/local "communities" in order to offer communitarian inclusion contra the alienating disaster of the presently existing economy—but also as a violent reaction against any sort of left-wing universalism. This is the defining feature of the far right's anti-communism.

It is not coincidental that groups like the Oath Keepers have veterans at their core, then. Brought together into tight-knit units by the demands of military life, soldiers experience an intensity of communal ties that is difficult to replicate under other conditions. Upon return, the absence of these ties easily turns into an existential void, as the soldier is not only cast out of their "tribe," but thrown back into the material community of capital, where devotion to such tribal units is considered not only backwards but even barbaric. The intensity of their experience marks them as outsiders to the palace of urban liberalism, but the necessity of living within the material community of capital forces them to do its bidding in order to survive. Many of these individuals—not only veterans but those who have experienced basic communal attachment through simple deprivation or religious upbringing— thereby adopt the traditional role of the warrior, simultaneously shunned by civilized society and necessary to its protection. The Norse martial-occultism of the Wolves of Vinland is not just a curious side-effect of their racial theories, then, but a concrete expression of their position at the walls of the palace. Getting jobs as security guards, first responders, or police officers, or simply play-acting in the militia or *volkisch* Odin cult are all duties taken with a bitter pride, the warrior patrolling the borders of the kingdom, facing the threats that the soft-handed city liberal simply cannot stomach. In Italy, the leader of the populist "Five Stars Movement" echoes Jack Donovan's call to "become a barbarian," praising the election of Trump with a new slogan: "It is those who dare, the obstinate, the barbarians who will take the world forward. We are the barbarians!"[27]

The Oath

In Nevada the real desert was not the dust or the sagebrush but the massive industrial leveling that characterizes the day-to-day functioning of a "healthy economy." The undead sagebrush at least held multitudes of life in its roots. Once, when one of my higher-ups had been out on a job, he'd run across a den of wild foxes. He spent several days watching them, counting their numbers, excited that the nearby mine hadn't driven away all the sparse desert fauna. But he made the mistake of telling his co-workers, and the next weekend one of the other employees— a red-faced, blundering man originally from some exurb in Florida—drove his truck out to the area, tracked down the foxes, shot them all, skinned them, and took the pelts as trophies. It often seems as if there is an unbridgeable gap between the minds of those enmeshed in the present world and those who see it as almost unthinkably monstrous, something that is not even a "world" but the name for an utterly atonal status quo constructed on the continual ruin of worlds as such. There are those who see foxes and those who see pelts.

The myth of the Third Position (the idea that people can and should take a political stance that goes "beyond left and right") comes from the observation that both the far right and the far left see the present world as untenable. They make no distinction between the fact that the far right is almost always dependent upon a mythic past to illustrate its illusion of order—whether national, tribal, filial, or simply some variant of the strong winning out over the weak—because their supposed "neither left nor right" politics is often founded on the same anthropological sleight of hand. For someone like Donovan, opposition to the present order is a call to "start the world." What this looks like, however, is a rather traditional masculine eco-tribalism, defined by the ability of men to become men again, the ability of white people to return to their "indigenous" roots, and the ability of local self-reliance to foster meritocracies in which the crippling effects of the present atonal order of status quo liberalism (poetically characterized as a "sky without eagles") is dissolved into local communitarian units defined by an organic hierarchy that ascends out of people's personal endowments, enhanced by training and discipline.

One day, while hiking around a dried-out wash to get at a particularly inaccessible stretch of fence, I also came across a den of foxes. Startled, one of them had shot out from the dark trellis of sagebrush to retreat across the flood bed, its paws scattering the rain-gathered stones. At some distance, it stopped and turned to look back at the threat from which it had fled. It met my eyes with its own, two dark pools as slick as oil, glinting with that wild light you can only catch for an instant, flashing across feral bodies like some force inside them writhing to get out, to spill into the world uncontained and that struggle itself driving the body forward, a glimpse of wilds untamed though plundered. In those eyes was a reminder that despite the mundane world-breaking driven by price and profit, worlds could still be born, linked together, made to bloom—that even when the economy seemed to have reached an unprecedented expanse, it was driven by a crisis that forced its very core constantly to decay, interstices opening within the cycles of accumulation and devastation. Wild, unpredictable potentials stirred in the desert. Insurrections shuddered out of the economy's roots like so many feral animals. Time seemed to slow, strung between myself and those glimmering eyes, both of us frozen, each seeming to expect something of the other. Then the fox turned and shot around the bend. I never saw it again. I never spoke of its existence.

Someone like Jack Donovan would also see the fox and not the pelt, maybe even seeing it much as I did. We might see the same economic apocalypse, the same increase in the valence of riots and insurrections, the same strategic openings offered by these events, the same placid misery offered by the status quo. But none of this makes us allies. The myth of the Third Position is precisely that opposition to the present order and all gradualist attempts to change it is the only unifying force that matters, with left and right being mere ideological accessories. But dig deeper and politics is inevitably replaced by nature, tradition, or some other seemingly apolitical order, in which the sanctity of the community is preserved by its ability to wall itself off from all others. Third Positionism, national anarchism, the Patriot Movement, and even the simple populism of Trump are all forms of blood politics. Political practice only exists for them insofar as it can be performed by kindred actors, and politics is the performance of this kinship.

What is nonetheless fascinating about the new far right is its commitment to pragmatic action. The Oath Keepers and Three Percenters offer a fundamental theoretical insight here, since their existence is dependent on the ability to unify across the fragmentation of the proletariat via the "oath" as a shared principle of action. In contrast to the unwieldy populism of "the 99%," the Patriot Movement proposes a focus on the functional abilities of an engaged minority (the "III%"), which can gain popular support via its ability to outcompete the state and other opponents in an environment of economic collapse. And it is this fact that is missed in most "anti-fascist" analysis. Rather than attempting to identify individual grouplets, parse their ideologies, and see how their practice accords (or doesn't) with whatever programs they've put forward (per the usual leftist formula), it is far more useful to explore moments like ours as chaotic processes in which many different actors have to take sides in relation to political upheavals, the collapse of the economic order, and the various new forces that arise amid all this. Such grouplets are often ad hoc, and frequently do not state any political positions. They seem empty of ideological content, or it is so vague as to be inconsequential. They are driven not by the program, but by the oath. The feature that distinguishes them is not so much their beliefs, as laid out in founding documents or key theoretical texts, but the way that they act relative to sequences of struggle and collapse. These are concrete things such as how they approach influxes of refugees and migrant workers, how they participate in (or against) local cycles of unrest, whom they ally themselves with in the midst of an insurrection, and whose interests they serve when they begin to succeed in the game of "competitive control," creating local structures of power.

The far right is defined by an oath of blood. They share the commitment to pragmatic action and the ability to see the untenable nature of the present economic order, but their actions are exclusionary, and their strategy envisions closed, communitarian solutions to systemic collapse. This is most visible in the more experienced, thought-out form of the Patriot Movement or the Wolves of Vinland, but it exists on a continuum, as more residents of the hinterland become aware of the apocalypse surrounding them. But the real political advance visible in the far right—and the thing that has made possible its recent ascendance—is the pragmatic focus on questions of power, which are religiously ignored by the American leftist, who instead focuses on building elaborate political programs and ornate utopias, as if politics were the exercise of one's imagination. It is this focus on building power in the midst of crisis that distinguishes the partisan from the leftist, and the oath is the present organizational form of partisanship.

Partisans

In more abstract terms, we can roughly schematize present political allegiances according to how they understand partisanship and position themselves relative to global sequences of struggle and insurrection. First, these global cycles of struggle are themselves the return of what Marx called the "historical party," which is essentially the name for the generalization of some degree of social upheaval across international boundaries, the increase in the rate at which new struggles become visible, and the intensity that they are able to reach. All struggles within the historical party tend toward what might be called "demandlessness," for lack of a better word. This isn't to say that individual struggles don't have particular demands, but that they tend actually to overflow with demands in such a way that the only thing that coheres them is a generalized rejection of the present order—the idea that all the politicians must go, that there just needs to be some fundamental change no matter its character, that the present cannot be borne any longer. This also often infers that they tend towards a generalized becoming-riot, since no simple suite of reforms can be pushed through, and all attempts to do so (via Syriza, Podemos, have ended in failure no matter their level of electoral success. It is through this demandlessness—the recognition in action that the present system is fundamentally impossible, rather than mismanaged—that the specter of communism is resurrected. The "invariant programme" of communism (a term used by Amadeo Bordiga, the leader of the Italian Communist Party in its insurrectionary heyday) is inferred by peoples' generalized action against the present, in which some sort of vaguely defined communalism is opposed to the material community of capital. But the specter only haunts the riot from its fringes, and the communal easily transforms into the communitarian.

In contrast, the "formal party" is the name for the emergence of organization from the motion of the historical party.

Organization here means the confrontation and overcoming of material limits to a given struggle. Whether those involved in this process think of themselves as in "an organization" is irrelevant. The reality is that such acts are unified more by the shared action implied by the oath, rather than card-carrying membership. Speaking of only the proto-communist partisans, Bordiga calls this the "ephemeral party," since its form and existence are contingent on historical conditions. Marx, mocking the fear-mongering press of the day, calls it the "Party of Anarchy." Whereas the historical party refers to content, the formal party refers, precisely, to pragmatic form—in this case the oath and the building of power—since it is positioned within a contingent array of historical conditions that require practical overcoming.

Bordiga and Marx both saw the union of the formal and historical parties as the emergence of the Communist Party proper. But there are also various forms of non-union between formal and historical party, in which individuals can play the role of anti-communist partisans—either in defense of the liberal status quo or as advocates of a reactionary alternative. In opposition to the "Party of Anarchy," Marx portrayed the alliance of ruling interests as a "Party of Order," since their conception of political upheavals was one that could see such events only as chaotic aberrations. These are individuals for whom the world is nothing but pelts, the economy a vast machine that unites the interests of humanity with that of capital. To be slightly more concrete, they are those urbanites who woke up on the morning after the election and looked around themselves in shock, as if someone had tied ropes around their ankles and dragged them out into the rust-spattered American bloodlands while they slept. Their expressions utterly ashen, they frantically tapped their phones trying to order an Uber to take them back home. But the Uber would never come. They earnestly could not conceive of a world in which Hillary had not won. How could people be so utterly crazy, they asked themselves, before scouring Facebook for a litany of responsible parties—racist ruralites, third-party voters, those infinitely troublesome anarchists, or that vast majority party in American politics: the faithless zealots of the "Did Not Vote" ticket. The Party of Order is defined by its desire that the riot or insurrection be simply smoothed over. They want reforms to be implemented. They want us to let the slow gears of justice turn. They want body cameras on cops. They want community policing. They don't see enough black faces in the room. They just want everyone at the table.

The Party of Order therefore opposes both the extreme left and the extreme right. For them, the problem is "extremism" as such, and the maintenance of the placid, atonal status quo. They have no politics, only administration. Donovan's characterization of liberalism as a "sky without eagles" is not an incorrect portrayal of their flattened world. The far right does, then, understand itself as opposed to the Party of Order, and may even conceive itself, broadly speaking, as part of the Party of Anarchy, since they also ride the tide of the historical party's upheavals, intervening in the same insurrections and wreaking destruction against the violent, mechanical order defended by global elites. But it is Donovan's solution to this atonality that hints at the true nature of the far-right position in an era of generalizing partisanship. His cure for atonality is an organically hierarchical Nietzschean tribalism, a return to some sort of primal indigeneity, encapsulated in the demand to "start the world." But what is the world he wants to start?

The formal parties of the far right are unable to fuse with the historical party because in essence they see the potentials opened by it as doors through which they might return to some sort of wholesome, organic order, which is opposed to both the anarchy of insurrection and the corrupt, false order of the status quo. For them, uprisings of the truly dispossessed are just as much symptoms of the system's decadence. Even while they draw from this anger, their politics is defined by its attempt simply to ignore the actual potentials offered by the historical party—to deny the specter of communism and execute its partisans. For them, these are only opportunities insofar as they are opportunities to hasten collapse. They thereby obscure politics as such, and thus it is natural that they claim to have moved "beyond left and right." Their practice is one that occults the potential for a communist response to the crisis, and their ideology is therefore not marked by any sort of consistent political program but by conspiracy and obfuscation. They don't see the historical party as foreboding a possible future at all, but instead as simply signaling the *return* of worlds amid the collapse of the world-shattering rituals of capital. The political event is obscured, the hastening of collapse replaces revolution, and wall-building preparation replaces communization. The far right is therefore neither the Party of Anarchy nor the Party of Order but the Anti-Party.

The political practice of the Anti-Party is centered on the masculinized practice of violence in the name of a wholesome, salvific order-to-come. In material terms, the far right tends to cluster among the interests of the petty proprietors or self-employed but still moderately wealthy workers of the hinterland. But the truth is that none of these phenomena have made country people inherently turn toward right-wing solutions, and the far hinterland is as much an ideological as material base for the far right. There was not even resounding support for Trump across the mud-soaked trailer parks and wind-swept mountain hamlets of the American hinterland, where most people simply did not vote. The material core of the far right is instead the whitening exurb, the actual home of most Patriots and Third Positionists, which acts as an interface between the metropolitan and non-metropolitan, allowing the wealthier landholders, business owners, cops, soldiers, or self-employed contractors to recruit from adjacent zones of abject white poverty, essentially funneling money from their own employment in urban industry into hinterland political projects.

Violence plays a central role here, since many of these individuals are active in the suppression of the surplus population in the near hinterland—the exurb bordering newly impoverished, diverse inner-ring suburbs where immigrants settle in large numbers alongside those forced out of the urban core by sky-rocketing rents. This reactionary politics is simply the idea that the regular violence used by the status quo in its maintenance of the present world of police, prisons, and poverty might also be widened, aimed at the urban core itself and the soft-handed liberals made to suffer. The world can be restored into the hands of the barbarians through salvific acts of violence, capable of forcing the collapse and hastening the approach of the True Community. It is in this way that the far right in the U.S., as elsewhere, is an essen-tially terroristic force, and will almost always target the innocent, the weak, and the dispossessed in its exercise of power. Behind the call to "start the world" lies a desire simply to watch it all collapse, to force the world to burn, and everyone to burn with it.

Drawing the Eagle from the Flesh

Stories changed hands in the trailer park like contraband. You were never sure of their source or their reliability, but everyone seemed to have an insatiable thirst for news of what was happen-ing in other mines, along the pipelines, out on the ranches, and amid the intricacies of the BLM bureaucracy. One story that stuck with me was about a miner in Golconda, that small town wedged between mines and farms, where workers would park their cars outside the bar in order to bus out to their work sites. No one knew what the guy was on, but everyone seemed to think it was more than whatever it seemed to be: some weed laced with something, some new sort of meth brought up by the cartels. Or it was angel dust, as if we were stuck in the fucking 1990s. Regardless of what he'd taken, the miner had gotten off his night shift and headed to that small bar in Golconda. The mines were worked in two shifts, day and night, each split between aboveground and underground work. You were paid the most for night work and for work underground, and that's what this miner did. He had some sort of condition, they said, a special sensitivity to light, like a vampire. He had to cover his skin in the desert sun or he'd start to burn, his flesh reddening and then bubbling up like the skin on an overcooked soup. So he worked nights and he worked underground, the farthest he could get from the light. This also meant that he made an enormous amount of money, ensuring that he could live comfortably for years after the boom had ended.

It was because of this fact that everyone assumed he must have been tweaking—he must have seen something in that haze of stimulants and just been broken by it. Because otherwise none of it made sense. He ran from the bar screaming incoherently, straight out into the midday light. Once outside, he ripped off his clothes as soon as the burning began, exposing the entirety of his nocturnal white body to that scorching, flesh-tearing avalanche of desert light, each ray reflected off the glass seizing into his pale skin like a meat hook. And he ran like that, naked, burning, smashing the windows of all the other miners' cars and throwing their belongings out into the sun with him. The sheriffs came eventually and tackled him into the dust, hardly able to get a grip on his shimmering, sun-boiled body. No one could understand whatever he was screaming. He just stared into the sun, yelling words that seemed not to be words—words occulted by the unspeakable sublimity of whatever salvation he'd seen through the drugs or through the simple misery of his lightless toil, all night digging into the hollowed earth, melting dust into gold for unimaginably rich men whom he would never see. They say that when they put the handcuffs on him his skin sloughed off like that of a snake, revealing the blood-red pulse of pure life like an incarnadine second body sitting beneath the first. That salvific, absolute body to come, maybe. The tribe, the nation, the ever-approaching community. The maddened eagle rising from the flesh.

two

Silver and Ash

The soil was blood red, heavy with iron and other ancient
metals gestated by the slow knotting and fissuring of tectonic
eons, now uplifted and ground apart by air, water and an invisible
chaos of microscopic life. It's often hard to connect the solidity
of earth and stone to their explosive origins, as pressure flays
subducted rocks down to their constituent chemicals and builds
them back stronger—all driven by that deep, distant rumbling of
the asthenosphere where solid stone flows like slow blood; this and
everything below just ripples in that constant, low-level explosion
atop which continents and ocean floor float like a fragile halo.
When the bomb went off, I don't remember seeing the combustion,
just the soil turned to red dust, small stones raining down into my
hair. Maybe the babysitter—in a fleeting moment of responsibility
wedged between making the bomb out of gunpowder and a plastic
coke bottle in the garage and lazily hurling it underhand into the
ridge like a softball—had covered our eyes, concerned about the
splinters of granite that might soon be bulleting toward us. Or
maybe explosions are sometimes just things you can't really see
entirely because they happen at a different scale than that to which
we're attuned, just as the tectonic crushing and flaying of minerals
to make this incarnadine earth is itself an explosion too slow to see.

It was sometime in the early to mid-1990s, when everything
had already begun to shake apart even as we were told that the

war for the world had finally been won. I always have trouble remembering my age in that interval between the end of the Cold War, when my first, muddiest memories were gathering, and the fall of the twin towers, when I was just beginning to hit puberty. Maybe it's just hard to think back to the End of History, a temporal glitch that was soon overcome as the wars and riots flooded in again. But maybe it's more that in the countryside there just wasn't much left to remember. Mining had collapsed long ago. Timber fell in pieces, starting with a plummet in the late 1970s, recovering to a lower plateau in the '80s, and then declining ever since.[1] Farming experienced the height of its crisis in the '80s, but in reality this was simply one period in a long decline in employment driven by mechanization.[2]

Unemployment wasn't the only thing left when the industries went. Loggers and miners had long used stimulants to stay awake for twelve-hour shifts of hard labor. When the mills and mines left, the meth didn't, and thus the crisis birthed the tweaker. I would only realize that this term is not ubiquitous much later, when a friend who had lived most of her life in the cities came to Oregon to work on a fire crew, where keeping itinerant tweakers out of makeshift camps was a regular task near any inhabited area. There is an entire art to it, really—the goal being not to get bitten, scratched or come into contact with tweaker blood, all while also not getting robbed. In recent years, the term has generalized with the drugs in fashion, shows like *Breaking Bad* bringing meth into primetime just as opiates were becoming the cutting-edge narcotic of choice in the countryside (before ketamine was a party drug, it was a common anesthetic for livestock, pets, and wildlife, after all). Tweaker demographics have changed somewhat over the years, but at the time, the term still referred specifically to white meth addicts.

The babysitter had what I would later come to recognize as tweaker eyes, bespeaking other explosions happening at other scales: the euphoric chemical explosion of dopamine and norepinephrine in the brain, the periodic explosion of meth labs in the forest like the sound of ancient trees finally being felled, the slow explosion of a rural way of life out into a groundless scattering of scams and desperate, private miseries. After a life mostly lived in the country, I am convinced that the eyes of tweakers see something that other eyes do not. Those orbs gouged deep down into their sockets like antlions awaiting prey, their presence only hinted at by that brief glint of quivering motion beneath the surface—as if the eyes are sunk straight back into the brain and thereby opened to some sort of neural augury, the iris black like a single, dilated pupil open to the world's many wounds and thus capable of seeing that world as it is: a congress of explosions tearing bodies apart all at different speeds and in different directions. This reality is a horror native to country people, accounting for our fascination with meth first and opiates second. One gives sight that reaches too far, illuminating monstrosities at the depth of a shattered world, and the other offers at last the consolation of a slow and quiet blinding.

Can I throw it next time? the son asked, and the father shook his head. You're still too young. The son, Bare, was my age, whatever that was, his nickname taken from his habit in winters of running outside and rolling around in the snow "bare-ass naked," as if he were trying to put out some sort of fire that had spread across the entirety of his body. When he played with toys, he would simply take one in each hand and smash them together as hard as he could until bits were flung off in every direction. I don't know what became of him after his parents went to jail. Before the dust had even settled, he was running into the small crater made by the explosion, as if magnetized to it. He returned from the dust cloud holding a small shard of the plastic bottle aloft, his face caked with ruddy soil fissured by streaks of sweat.

Tweakers have become objects of revulsion within rural America, not due to their many moral failures or seemingly

plague-ridden bodies but because of their matter-of-fact
recognition that those of us from the country are all already
dead. The way of life has been destroyed in a devastating,
irrevocable fashion, essential industries torn out from under
us, ecosystems razed, and everyone left suffering not just
material deprivation but an expansive social and cultural
collapse that can only be characterized as apocalyptic. The
many new non-denominational Christian sects that sprang up
in the early stages of this collapse offered a simple solution for
the dead: to become born again. But now even these sects are
shrinking as people see what the tweakers' heresy had perceived
all along: the born again are born dead or die soon after through
the thousand sacrificial cuts of daily drudgery. The rapture of
apocalypse is therefore not on its way but instead long past.
We're adrift in its wake.[3]

As even the new Christian sects collapse, a vacuum is left at
the social core of the small towns and expansive counties that
compose rural America. This vacuum has not yet been filled, but
the tweaker is in a way a vanguard of whatever's coming. And this
vanguard is neither inherently right wing nor left wing, despite
the long-standing affinity between Nazis and amphetamines. The
tweaker instead represents the most basic recognition of the ways
in which the far hinterland has been made futureless, an organic
nihilism emerging from the American countryside, unprecedented
and unpredictable. I turned my head from the crater and the soil-
streaked child to gaze out beyond the old timber road cut into
the red dirt of the ridgeline, across second-and-third generation
forests barely recovered from a century of constant denudation.
In the distance, you could see a spattering of small clearings
where people gardened or grew weed, their small figures just
barely visible, shuffling between ant-like herds of livestock and
labyrinths of gutted trucks and tractors. Explosions form a sort of
foundational ritual here because they match the tweaker's vague
recognition with an equally vague hope: the sense that cataclysm

is a thing that can be built and not just suffered under, that it might be possible for people living in the wake of a world-breaking apocalypse to build their own forms of spectacular violence. Not striving to become born again or build another, better world, but just to force the end of this one to go all the way up.

Armies of Mud and Flame

I was raised in the mountains overlooking a small river valley in a mildly secessionist border territory stretched between Oregon and California. Distant from the administrative centers of either state, the area seems to be governed more by a congress of floods, fires, and other forces of nature. In the depths of the Klamath Mountains, alpine snowmelt winds down narrow cuts of granite into storm-fattened rivers that writhe through the valley bottoms like blue-green eels. Black bears hibernate in hidden, snow-sealed grottoes. Elk brush their broad antlers through the soft-needled bowery of fir and pine. In spring, rainstorms and thawing frost dislodge entire ridgelines from the mountains, periodically feeding roads, houses, and rich-smelling groves of evergreen into the endless maw of churning water. Everyone seems to know someone who was sacrificed to those grand, deadly rivers—the Klamath, the Rogue, the Trinity.

The region's mountain geography has its social counterpart. Upriver means mostly white valley towns encircled by alfalfa, with farms and ranches stretched up into the foothills. It means church, school, post office—the places where power seems to touch down from afar, if only gently. Downriver, on the other hand, is a violent land speckled with mud-sunken trailers, over-grown trailheads, secretive mansions built by weed barons, and ramshackle hamlets beyond the reach of any highway. Farms give way to forest service substations and, farther still, the tribal lands and reservations along the rivers' lower reaches. Downriver is where the waters converge. Any corpse dumped upstream will finally surface there, bobbing and circling in eddies where the rivers mix. It's a land that's hardly land, more a swirl of water and roots helmed by storms—a place where dark stories grow into ponderous myths overlooking the timbered ruin.

It has the uncanny feel of an almost-foreign country. The downriver towns are painted with tribal symbols or fly the libertarian flag of the State of Jefferson, emblazoned with a gold pan and two Xs, signifying that we've been "double-crossed" by the government. In the 1970s and '80s, a series of communes were set up along the Salmon and the Klamath by back-to-the-land hippies convinced that America was a soulless empire on the verge of collapse. The deep folds of oak and evergreen were to be a site of spiritual rebirth, a catchment for refugees from a dying nation. But over the space of a decade, the empire refused to die, and each of the communes fell instead, evacuated of everything but their guns and drugs. Now those who are left simply curse the state for wanting to flood the valleys to siphon more water to the cities in the south. Along the river roads, meth-stricken sawyers set up small stands selling burl statues of bears and hunched, grim-looking sasquatch.

In summer, wildfires sparked in the unpopulated interior burst forward like an invading army. Clearcutting had led to mass replanting of trees, and property protection had encouraged widespread fire prevention, all ensuring that the regrown forest would be neither staggered in its growth nor properly thinned. Meanwhile, deadfall would accumulate unhindered, new seeding of fire-symbiont evergreens would be slowed, and the natural firebreak offered by oak savanna gradually closed. The feedback is essentially the same as that between bubble, crisis, and stimulus in today's economy: all of this leads to larger, less containable wildfires, which of course increase the demand for fire prevention and thereby increase the risk and severity of future wildfires. As the bubble gets bigger, so does the coming crisis, and even bigger debt-financed stimulus is required to combat it when it hits, laying the ground for the next crisis, ever larger than the first. There is no final crisis, just the continual management of widening collapse.

Individual disaster industries tend to rapidly become self-sufficient, predicated on an underlying, secular increase in the scope and scale of their devastation. But the greater the devastation, the greater the resources required for its management. In late summer, yellow-clad wildland firefighters flood into the many hidden valleys of the Trinity Alps, the Marble Mountains, and the Kalmiopsis Wilderness, where they fight the invading flames in a series of defensive battles that invariably end in defeat. Afterwards everything is laid to waste, the earth char-black, yellow shirts and green pants dimmed under a gray silk of ash. Nonetheless, it's one of the few decent-paying jobs that can be found in the area—no small matter in places like Trinity County, California, which reached almost 20 percent unemployment at the height of the last crisis. The firefighters therefore tend to be ruralites drawn from different parts of the greater region, sometimes deployed a county over and at other times called to quell far-off infernos rolling through the North Cascades or Coeur d'Alenes. All ultimately paid for by federal money, the industry is cut into an ornate hierarchy defined by proximity to this source of funding, which translates into intricate divisions of labor and status on the ground. The most privileged strata of workers are those employed directly by the Forest Service (or the BLM, in states like Nevada). They are generally the best-paid and best-equipped crews, and their status is marked both by their vehicles' insignia and by more minor social signals such as the way that their gloves are affixed to their uniform. The contract crews, on the other hand, are a far more flexible labor force employed by private companies that compete to win federal contracts. Since these crews are only deployed when there's a fire, the Forest Service doesn't have to incur the costs of maintaining them across the entire season.

If timber and ore were the gods of the old west, fire and flood are the gods of the new one. With little to replace collapsed productive industries, the last few decades have seen the region become more and more dependent upon government funding, all the surrounding counties essentially mirroring the predicament of Josephine County described in the previous chapter. Much of this funding is poured into agencies such as respective state Departments of Transportation, which help to repair the massive stretches of roads that are destroyed by landslides every season—again, often through baroque systems of subcontracting. Natural disaster (rarely "natural" in any real sense) is one of the only industries left, and rural areas have adapted to exploit this last, desperate economic opportunity. Nowhere is this clearer than in wildland firefighting and the transformation of the Forest Service:

> In 1991, fire suppression accounted for about 13 percent of the agency's budget, but by 2012 it made up more than 40 percent. Frequently, this hasn't been enough to cover fire suppression, and in recent years the agency has regularly overspent. After burning through its fire suppression budget [in 2013], the agency announced in August that it was cutting $600 million in other areas of its work, to fund firefighting, leading some to disparagingly refer to it as the "Fire Service."[4]

This trend only intensified in subsequent years. By 2015, fire suppression consumed 52 percent of the budget, and the Forest Service itself projects that by 2025 that number will rise to a staggering 67 percent, essentially completing the wholesale transformation of the agency. This has already been accompanied by a complete inversion in agency employment, with fire staffing more than doubling in size to compose the majority of Forest Service jobs, while the number of non-fire staff has been halved. Moreover, this number doesn't count the numerous outside contractors employed during fire season.[5] The coincidence of mass drought, poor management, and a desperate need for jobs have all combined to more or less guarantee the replacement of an old land management agency by a quasi-military Fire Service capable of offering at least a minimal level of employment amid economic devastation.

When fires do break out, much of the immediate area takes on the character of a war zone. Mass evacuations are accompanied by the establishment of Incident Command Centers surrounded by a constellation of forward-operating bases from which teams of firefighters can be deployed to defend key assets and establish a coherent front against the oncoming blaze. Kevlar-clad sawyers tear into the forest like a barbarian horde hacking its way through some monstrous enemy. Swampers scurry back and forth, clearing the sawyers' trail of devastation—all an orchestrated chaos designed to cut a line capable of starving the fire of its fuel. The logic and the methods are essentially military, and draw heavily from both the logistics and theory of contemporary counter-insurgency operations. Fire crews are relatively disaggregated small teams of specialists deployed to combat not only a concrete enemy but the very environment from which it draws its power. The goal is not really victory but containment, attrition, and the continual management of a war that never ends. Many contract crews are run by veterans, and the Forest Service itself often partners with the military, even using Air Force equipment and deploying active Army and Marine units to fight on the fire lines.[6]

While funding is funneled through federal agencies such as the Forest Service or BLM, most wildland firefighters are on contract crews, in which they tend to make less than $1,000 a week for continuous stretches of seven-day weeks (technically fourteen days is the maximum before at least two days off are required, but this is often extended), and even then they are likely only working for a few months out of the year, if that. The work, of course, is immensely dangerous. In 2013 a rapidly moving wildfire near Yarnell, Arizona, overcame a team of firefighters on a local crew,

killing nineteen. This crew was an elite "hotshots" team funded
by local and state government, all of its members experienced
and well equipped. Contract crews, on the other hand, are often
under-supplied and usually operated as a minor warlord fiefdom
might be, one's fate determined by the whim of crew commanders
and the bosses above.

But in these places, any pay is good pay. According to the
USDA's Economic Research Service, almost all the counties that
compose the California–Oregon border region are either "Federal-
state Government-dependent" or "Nonspecialized." Across the
entire nation, counties in these categories already had the lowest
median incomes and the highest poverty rates on average out of
all rural counties prior to 2008. They saw an even further drop in
incomes and an increase in poverty during the height of the crisis.
But, more importantly, they also never experienced a substantial
bounce-back during the "recovery." Instead, incomes simply kept
dropping for four years, finally flatlining and then inching up
ever-so-slightly after 2013/14 but never regaining their previous
(already extremely low) levels. Similarly, poverty rates still sit
some two to three percentage points higher than their already-
high pre-recession levels.[7]

Those working the line know there are few other options.
Most are not local to the area, but the vast majority tends to
come from the same global hinterland. After working a season
on a crew in Idaho, Lennon Bergland, a journalist writing for
Vice, confirms this, explaining that his coworkers "come from a
range of places and backgrounds, but most have spent at least
part of their lives at the edge of society, in broken homes plagued
with abusive families and drugs."[8] Though many are drawn from
the bottom rungs of the white population, the fire crew, like most
workplaces in the hinterland, tends to be far more diverse than
one might presume. Bergland describes one crew member born
in Medellín, Colombia, but raised by Mormons in Idaho, hoping
to earn enough money from the season to travel to Colombia and

find his family. A growing number are also inmates, especially in California, where some 30 to 40 percent of all wildland firefighters are prisoners—mostly low-level felons who have volunteered to join a "conservation camp," in which they are paid $2 a day while in the program and $2 an hour when on the line.[9] But Bergland also captures the image of a typical, non-inmate firefighter in his crew in western Idaho:

> Hans is one of the few men with a family. He grew up in the white supremacist-dominated section of Northern Idaho, poor, with an asshole step-father who later killed himself with a shotgun. Hans used to go to the woods every fall with a buddy, a case of beer, and a chainsaw to harvest lodge pole pines to sell for firewood. He is by far the hardest worker on the crew, smiling constantly and telling stories about hunting, fighting, and getting in trouble with the Idaho police. He is working to pay for the chemotherapy for his six-year-old daughter with Leukemia.[10]

This is but one of many similar stories that populate the war zone workplaces of the far hinterland, where productive industries have largely been replaced by an ever-losing battle against our epoch's colliding catastrophes.

Hidden Temples

Traveling along the Klamath, you get a sense of everything slowly turning upside down. The river is born in the lava-scorched plains of southern Oregon, where irrigated flatlands are intercut with volcanic ridgelines marking the eon-slow movement of strato-volcanoes across the landscape. As it rolls westward, the placid, pesticide-polluted river cuts into the slowly uplifting Klamath Mountains, where the water is filtered through the mazelike channels of granite and diorite until the downstream rapids grow clearer than those of the watershed—a river turned upside down. Population decreases, and the arid, volcanic landscape gives way to a labyrinthine geology in which relatively young sedimentary deposits might be intercut with ancient, subducted metamorphic rocks and outcroppings of black and rust-red peridotite ejected from the dark blood-churn of the mantle far below. Even the strata must often be read in reverse, the oldest layers twisted by tectonics until they sit above or astride younger ones. And atop everything teems a stunning chaos of flora and fauna, sunk tooth and root into the landscape. Plant life fails to follow the orderly altitude models seen in other mountainous regions. This and many other curiosities have led scientists to think of the area not so much as a single ecosystem but as a "knot," where many landscapes have been tied together, piled upside down, one on top of the other, their origins occulted.[11]

It's also here that white, rural America begins to be turned on its head. Many parts of the far hinterland are as cosmopolitan as any city, and always have been. Rural diversity is simply more dispersed and more segregated. There are hints of this buried in all the mountain towns of the West. Weaverville, located just off the Trinity River, houses one of the last remaining Taoist temples in the region, and one of the oldest Chinese temples in California. The Weaverville Joss House (named The Temple Among the Trees and Beneath the Clouds in Chinese) was built in 1874 to replace an even earlier temple that had burned down. Today it houses numerous mining artifacts used by Chinese immigrant workers and antique weapons from the Tong Wars—a period of internecine conflict and defensive violence within u.s. Chinese settlements, centered on San Francisco's Chinatown and coinciding roughly with a stretch of economic depression and rising anti-Chinese sentiment. Such temples, often the center of vibrant Chinatowns, once dotted the landscape of the far West. But following wave upon wave of mass deportations (often carried out by nativist mobs), the Chinatowns were gradually demolished.

Today it's still common for people excavating old plots to find the remnants of foundations and hidden tunnels built by the Chinese—some say for smuggling; others say for escaping anti-Chinese pogroms.

Farther down the Klamath and the Trinity lie California's largest reservations, the Hoopa and Yurok, with a patchwork of smaller tribal lands and use-rights given to the Karuk and Klamath as well. Such spaces offer a glimpse of maybe the most systematically ignored segment of the American underclass. Some of the highest shares of poverty in the U.S. are found not in the "inner city," but instead within rural counties with predominantly black, Hispanic and indigenous populations, as well as in the poorest parts of white Appalachia. According to the 5-Year American Community Survey for 2015, the ten counties with the highest share of population in poverty were all "majority-minority" rural counties located in places such as the predominantly black Mississippi Delta, the largely Hispanic Texas borderlands, or the areas around reservations such as Pine Ridge, in South Dakota. After these come the historically poor Appalachian counties, and then the urban ones.[12] Comparing urban to rural shares of poverty by race, rural areas come out on top for every category. As measured by the Census' admittedly archaic race and ethnicity categories: Though the poverty rate for black urbanites already sits at 26 percent, averaged across all urban counties, the same rate for black ruralites rises to 36.9 percent. American Indians see the next highest shares, at 25.4 percent urban and 33 percent rural.[13]

The same pattern exists for the Hispanic population, with 23.9 percent in poverty in urban areas and 27.5 percent in rural.[14] But this number is suspiciously low, likely due to the fact that the Census often provides slightly less accurate population data in some rural areas due to the large influx of undocumented immigrants working on farms, mines, pipelines, or the new oil fields in places like North Dakota. Though such immigrants compose only 4.8 percent of the total rural population, they are predominantly concentrated in the Southwest and in a handful of rural counties in the Pacific Northwest and the South. In Washington and Oregon, many of the counties with the highest shares of foreign-born people are in rural, farming-dependent parts of the state. The same is becoming true for places like Georgia and North Carolina, as more restrictive immigration laws push migrants to new destinations in the South to work in agriculture, food processing, or manufacturing.[15] These are low-paying jobs, with unrest met by threats of deportation. One of the few studies of poverty among immigrants in rural areas found that the poverty rate for rural, non-citizen immigrants sat at 31.6 percent, compared to 13.7 in urban areas. While other groups' poverty rates skyrocket due to un- and underemployment, 15.6 percent of rural immigrants tend to be in poverty even when working full time, compared to 8 percent for native-born ruralites.[16]

These populations often disappear in images of rural America due to a combination of geography, segregation, and low population density. Despite the historical diversity of the countryside and its rapid rate of change, whites remained a disproportionate majority at 77.8 percent of all rural population in 2010, compared to a national share of 63.7 percent in that same year.[17] Historically, rural areas segregated at the same rate as urban ones—a phenomenon especially strong in the South.[18] And contemporary patterns of rural segregation have continued to roughly match their urban counterparts, with the black population experiencing the highest levels of segregation between 1990 and 2000.[19] After 2000, there is evidence that Hispanic segregation rates in "new destinations" such as the South and Pacific Northwest grew even more rapidly, though the rate varied substantially with local economic conditions.[20]

Overall, this segregation ensures that substantial segments of the far hinterland remain largely white spaces, and it is these areas that tend to dominate popular perceptions of rural life. Geographically, the dominance is uneven. Whites compose the vast majority (more than 90 percent) of the share of total rural population in the northeastern Rust Belt, the Midwest, and much of the Corn Belt. Many Mountain and Pacific Northwest states see this number drop to 70 or 80 percent, but the concentration of the minority population in a handful of farming counties or hard-to-reach tribal lands still guarantees that much of the countryside appears almost exclusively white at first glance. In the South, this appearance begins to falter, much of the far hinterland cut into a patchwork of long-segregated swamps, forests, and small towns. Here, the white rural population averages about 60 percent, ranging from higher shares in the Appalachian states to the lowest share in South Carolina, at 56.5 percent white and 36.4 percent black. In the Southwest, such reversals become the norm. Rural California is only 54.4 percent white, Arizona is 57.5 percent, and Texas is 58.4 percent. The trend reaches its apex in New Mexico, where the rural population is only 38.6 percent white.[21]

Currencies

In 1964 severe floods tore trees from the shores of the Klamath and sent the timber crashing through downriver bridges as landslides washed away stretches of highway. Overnight, the entire region was transformed into an archipelago of isolated islands, accessible only by air and sea. People still speak proudly of the floods today, as an exhibit of the area's supposed self-reliance. And much of the region remains loosely connected to the global infrastructure of modern states and supply chains. For years the entirety of the Internet in coastal Humboldt County ran through a single cord stretched southward to the Bay Area via Highway 101. When severed by landslides, road crews, or oblivious farmers, tens of thousands would lose Internet access, landlines would be inoperable, and credit cards would become useless sheaves of plastic.

And the bottlenecks were not exclusively virtual: before 101 was straightened in southern Humboldt, the "Redwood Curtain" even ensured that goods trucked into coastal range would have to be transferred to smaller vehicles capable of navigating the narrow highways, creating local inflation bubbles in the price of gas and staple foodstuffs. In its own strange way, this bottleneck acted as a sort of physical trade tariff, creating greater price parity for producers who were behind the "Redwood Curtain" and increasing demand for their products. Traveling even farther inland from the "Lost Coast" into the heart of the Klamaths, the otherwise pervasive totality of states and markets appears upended, everything given over to a sort of casual anarchy. A friend who used to truck furniture from the coast to the Hoopa reservation had to navigate not by address but by kinship networks and word of mouth—and even then the final destination of any good was often unreachable, located beyond narrow trails or impassable roads. Meanwhile, government is devolved down to the bare skeleton of administration: tribal councils and cash payments allotted by quanta of blood.[22]

But real rural autonomy is an illusion. The state never just recedes. Wildland firefighters offer one image of its persistence, even the social arm of government tending to take a martial form in the outer orbits of power. But in the depths of California's "Emerald Triangle," a more direct symbol of that city-ensconced state comes in the form of the dark, military helicopters that buzz like wasps through the snow-capped wilderness. Though most often conducting reconnaissance for ground crews, the helicopters would sometimes pitch and arc with the added weight of heavily armed mercenaries. At these times, you knew that the machines were bound somewhere, preparing to settle into alpine meadows where paramilitary soldiers would spill out across the warm summer fields to pull people from their houses at gunpoint, drag them across the wildflowers, and destroy their crops in front of their eyes.[23]

Many of the official economic statistics gathered in these areas are deceptive. When jobs evaporate, but people are still forced to buy food on the market and pay off taxes, rent, and their many debts, the economy is actually in a state of impartial collapse. In such conditions, black and gray markets emerge to fill the vacuum. The "nonspecialized" or government-dependent counties of the aspirational State of Jefferson are in reality dependent on a new, informal economic base. In part, this is composed of hobbled-together scams, diverse in their character and degree of illegality. The year I graduated high school, a friend of a friend in Yreka, California, was busted for running a virtual liquor store, stealing alcohol from his part-time job at the 76 near the freeway and selling it on Myspace. Over in Humboldt County, a roommate of mine worked several years for a local scrapping, hauling, and landscaping company run by an old libertarian who swore that Obama was a Kenyan socialist, hired mostly ex-cons, and paid everybody in locally minted silver coins. Every morning in Humboldt Bay the docks were covered with people fishing or drawing in crab cages. In the mountains, venison and salmon acted as minor currencies. I often worked clearing the forest around the property of local landowners, paid cash to oversee controlled burns in the hope that their houses might be marginally safer when the fires passed through. Hunting, fishing, odd jobs, and minor theft—these made up the employment profile of the region.[24]

Though the numbers remain hazy, the *legal* portion of the nationwide "shadow economy" (such as the under-the-table jobs listed above) had an output of around a trillion dollars in 2009, or about 8 percent of U.S. GDP at the time. This legal shadow economy is rapidly growing,[25] but the truly dominant industries in many of these areas were all illegal, at least under federal law. The numbers that are available for black- and gray-market commerce are clearest for marijuana, which has existed in a littoral zone between local or partial legality and federal illegality for decades. Even prior to recreational legalization, the available data suggested that marijuana was the biggest cash crop in several states, including California, and likely one of the biggest cash crops in the country.[26] In northern California and southern Oregon, weed coexisted with local start-ups in meth[27] and, later, opiates,[28] which themselves compose the economic base of many rural counties where the climate (whether meteorological or political) is not well suited to large weed plantations. The black- and gray-shadow economy is not entirely drug-related, however. In rural areas along the u.s.–Mexico border, for example, smuggling constitutes a substantial employment base for local economies. And, despite an entire genre of gothic, borderland narco-journalism implying otherwise, most smuggling is in fact not drug trafficking, but rather the mundane, if illegal, concealed transport of consumer goods across the border to avoid customs payments.[29] Whatever its composition, this shadow base is then accompanied by a bloating in induced demand within real estate and the service sector, where black market wages are laundered into the formal economy.

Not all rural counties are primarily dependent on the shadow economy, though the informal sector does tend to comprise a larger share of their employment, on average.[30] Overall, however, most regions still depend on just one or two industries. Out of all rural counties in the u.s., "nonspecialized" compose the largest single share, at 29.6 percent, and are not distributed in any particular pattern. In general, however, the official economy of the hinterland is still far more dependent on goods-producing industries such as farming (19.8 percent of all counties), manufacturing (17.8 percent), and mining (9.3 percent). Government-dependent counties have overtaken mining-dependent ones at 12 percent, and recreation-dependent counties make up the second-lowest share, at 11.5 percent.

Manufacturing in rural areas tends to be concentrated in the northeast and Midwest, farming in the Plains states and Corn Belt, and mining in several clusters concentrated in Nevada, West Virginia, the Rocky Mountain states, and in the oil fields of Texas and the Dakotas. Government and recreation dependency are also widely distributed, but tend to be more concentrated in the far west as well as in the u.s.–Canada borderlands in the Midwest and Maine.[31]

The far hinterland is a sparsely settled expanse of grass- and grainlands, where oil pipelines cut across the landscape like black scars. It's a fundamentally inconsistent terrain, but also one in which ruined mountain hamlets, desert trailer parks, cookie-cutter cornfields, and bayou towns are united by an uncanny feeling of similarity—there are really only so many ways to kill a place. Aside from the informality and illegality of their employment profiles and the tendency to rely on productive or extractive industries, they are also united by a certain feeling of slowing time, days stretched long and empty by unemployment, hollowed mills and factories pieced apart by the concrete-wrenching roots of grass and shrubbery. If such a feeling can be given any more analytic definition, it probably lies in the simple fact that much of the far hinterland has a low economic output compared to both the suburban near hinterland and the metropolitan core. This sort of slowness gets to you, sinking into your body and wrapping itself like molasses around your bones. The longer you stay, the harder it becomes to reach the velocity needed to escape.

Plagues

This divergence in economic activity is only beginning to take political shape. A hint of it was finally visible in the 2016 election, when that vast terra incognita dubbed "Trump Country" was finally sighted from the twin peninsulas of liberal America. The economic character of the divergence could not have been more clear: Clinton almost universally carried the high-output metropolitan counties, comprising "a massive 64 percent of America's economic activity as measured by total output in 2015," while "Trumpland consists of hundreds and hundreds of tiny low-output locations that comprise the non-metropolitan hinterland of America, along with some suburban and exurban metro counties." Altogether, "Trump's supporting counties generated just 36 percent of the country's output." Trump's most politically active base was in wealthier exurbs, and in the counties of the far hinterland he was carried to the presidency more by rising shares of non-voters than by any sort of active support. Nonetheless, his election signals this greater divide, and "for a losing presidential candidate to have represented so large a share of [the] nation's economic base . . . appears to be 'unprecedented in the era of modern economic statistics.'"[32] Despite being a rich urbanite whose occupation is little more than the pouring of inherited wealth into gaudy, gilded palaces, Trump himself has become a sort of strange, terrifying specter of the starved heartland, a golden-fleshed death god summoned by deindustrialization, his distance from this devastation a mark of his own grim divinity.

There is a strong, probably congenital desire in American liberalism to blame such conservative political turns on some deeply ingrained ignorance bred into people by the soil and water of the heartland. The election of Trump was no exception, and the normal accusations ran their course through the encyclopedia of rural degeneracy before turning, finally, to that good, trusted enemy of the American polity: Russia and her allies. However disparaging, this process did at least return some attention to the question of white poverty in the u.s., so religiously ignored by those on the left. While rural America is clearly not synonymous with whiteness, it remains true that whites still compose a massive share of both the national and rural populations, and rural areas see some of the most extreme examples of poverty among all racial groups. Because of the extremity of the crisis in the far hinterland, the area also acts as a sort of window into the future of class conflict in the United States. The resulting image, however, is not the one favored by the metropolitan think piece, which sees racial resentment as the natural outcome of such "economic anxiety." Instead, traditional methods of transforming class antagonism into racial difference are beginning to reach a sort of saturation point, as unemployment, mortality, and morbidity rates all start to overspill their historically racial boundaries. The effects of this are extremely unpredictable, and political support will tend to follow whomever can offer the greatest semblance of strength and stability.

But the left is neither strong nor stable. Liberals ignore these areas because low-output, low-population regions very simply do not matter much when it comes to administering the economy—and that is, in the end, what liberalism is about. The far left, on the other hand, has long been in a state of widespread degeneration. It has retreated from historic strongholds in the hinterland (such as West Virginia, once a hotbed for wildcat strikes and communist organizing) to cluster around the urban cores of major coastal cities and a spattering of college towns. One symptom of this more widespread degeneration has also been an inward turn, mass organizing replaced by the management of an increasingly minuscule social scene and politics itself reenvisioned as the cultlike repetition of hollow rituals accompanied by the continual, self-flagellating rectification of one's words, thoughts, and interpersonal interactions. Theoretical rigor has atrophied, and the majority within the amorphous social scene that composes "the left" only vaguely understand what capitalism is. This condition tends to blur the border between left and right, as both will offer solutions that lie somewhere between localist communitarianism and protectionist development of the "real economy."

Another symptom is the neurotic obsession with anatomizing oppression and the assumption that revolutionary activity must originate from the "most oppressed" within a population. Class war and the revolutionary potentials that can be opened by it are inherently contingent—there is no "revolutionary subject" out there waiting to be discovered by leftist bloggers. To the extent that there is a correlation between one's experience of oppression and one's openness to revolution, it tends to be a non-linear probability distribution, with the highest probability lying not among the "most oppressed" but among the groups who, for whatever reason, had experienced some degree of prolonged improvement in their condition followed by a sudden, sharp reversal.[33] In certain ways, this describes the post-Civil-Rights experience of the black population, seemingly advanced by desegregation and the growth in home ownership, all capped by the rise of a not-insubstantial black ruling class and the election of Barack Obama—this "postracial" America was, of course, quickly proven hollow, as the housing crash dispossessed black homeowners, mass incarceration increased in scope, and extrajudicial killings of black youth skyrocketed. The political significance of this will be explored in later chapters. But what is often not acknowledged is that poor whites tend to have experienced a similar curve in their prospects, despite the absolute difference in their degree of social power. Young white workers, after all, have some of the lowest probabilities of ever doing better than their parents, even while they are on average much better educated—and it is these relative reversals that tend to have the strongest subjective effects.

Maybe most importantly, whites still compose an unarguably substantial portion of the American proletariat, even if the "white working class" is essentially an empty signifier. Poverty data, while an inadequate stand-in for the complexities of class position, nonetheless offers some insight. While the *share* of whites below the poverty line is consistently lower compared to other groups (though shares for all are higher for ruralites), in absolute numbers whites still compose the largest single group living in poverty in the United States, at 17.98 million family-units, or 41.3 percent of the total number (43.5 million) of families under the poverty line. They are followed by the Hispanic population, at 12.23 million (28 percent of total in poverty), and the black population, at 9.6 million (21 percent). In the rural core of white poverty, centered in Appalachia (but also with significant swaths in the Rust Belt and Pacific Northwest), the statewide share of whites living under the poverty line can reach as high as 17 percent (in Kentucky)—and again, while the share is much higher for the black (36 percent) and Hispanic (42 percent) population, the 646,800 white families living under the poverty line in Kentucky account for 74.3 percent of the state's poor.[34]

Alongside poverty come higher rates of unemployment, imprisonment, and drug use, and skyrocketing mortality and morbidity rates. The county that sends the most people to prison per capita (often with much longer sentences than elsewhere) is largely white Dearborn County, Indiana, with 114 prison admissions per 10,000 residents. But the phenomenon is not limited to any peculiarity of this blindingly white Indiana exurb. Imprisonment rates in small counties (those with fewer than 100,000 people) have been growing rapidly nationwide for the past decade, overcoming the rates in midsized and populous counties sometime between 2008 and 2009, and all without any comparable increase in crime.[35] Part of this shift can be attributed to the recent adoption of mass incarceration as a political issue by urban liberals, sparked by best-selling exposés such as Michelle Alexander's *The New Jim Crow*, which has led to a welcome decrease in the incarceration rate within most major American cities, including a substantial decrease in the incarceration rate among the black population. But the curious counterpart to this phenomenon has been an increase in the incarceration rate among whites. Though still disproportionately small compared to the rate experienced by the black, Native, or Hispanic populations, it has been steadily rising over the past decade—the starkest increase being among white women, among whom the rate rose some 56 percent between 2000 and 2014.[36]

The same rural areas that have been rapidly increasing their incarceration rates are also those that have seen skyrocketing rates of drug addiction and overdose deaths over the past twenty years. In Stark County, Ohio (almost 89 percent white), so many people have overdosed on opiates that local morgues have had to order cold storage trailers just to contain all the corpses.[37] The overdose death rate is so high that the CDC is now comparing it to the peak of the HIV epidemic, but whereas HIV deaths were far more concentrated in cities, the last decade's spike in overdoses is visible in both urban and rural areas, with the rural rate jumping above the urban beginning in the mid-2000s. Today, some of the highest overdose rates are found in rural Appalachia and the Southwest. The phenomenon thereby spans the rural racial divide, with some of the strongest concentrations of overdose deaths in West Virginia and New Mexico, states that have completely opposite shares of rural white population.[38]

And drug overdoses compose only one portion of a startlingly fast increase in the death rate among rural whites, even while death rates for all other groups continue to fall. In fact, increasing death rates tend to be extremely uncommon in developed countries short of war or substantial political and economic collapse.[39] As with the poverty rate, whites on average still tend to have lower overall death rates than other groups, but this increasing mortality and morbidity is, again, something experienced by a substantial number of people. And in certain respects, even the larger racial pattern is beginning to reverse: "In at least 30 counties in the South, black women in midlife now have a lower mortality rate than middle-aged white women."[40] The trend spans genders and age groups, but is strongest among those with only a high-school education, among whom the reversal is remarkable: "Death rates for white non-Hispanics with a high-school education or less now exceed those of blacks overall."[41] Especially prominent is the spiking mortality among older workers with only a high school diploma, among whom the death rate is "30% higher for whites age 50 to 54 than for blacks overall of that age."[42] Alongside drug overdoses, suicide and cirrhosis of the liver have led the increase in mortality. While the increase appears most clearly in the states with the poorest rural areas, it is not directly correlated with any rise in the poverty rate over the same period of time.[43]

If history is any indicator, the social plagues that gestate in the swamps and wastelands of the rural fringe eventually make their way to the gates of the palace. Death, addiction, and imprisonment feed into that apocalyptic atmosphere, the population teetering somewhere between sorrow, apathy, and rage. But rural whites won't just die off, as much as urban liberals might prefer such an outcome. Instead, the plague gives flesh to the mythology of the far right. These skyrocketing deaths seem to offer a concrete character, however fleeting and inaccurate, to the old white nationalist claim that white people are somehow being systematically killed. Of course, the phenomenon has none of the conspiratorial airs that the far right imagines, and in most areas whites still retain a strong structural advantage in access to education, healthcare, and all the other factors that contribute to lower mortality and greater well-being. It is nonetheless notable that the divergence in mortality between whites with only a high-school diploma and (largely urban) whites with college educations is now greater than the divergence between the average rate for the black population and those same college-educated whites.

This has created a situation in which none of the components of what liberals like to call "privilege" are necessarily visible from the depths of mountain poverty in the Appalachians or the Klamaths. Individuals might be raised by opiate-addicted parents; work ugly, deadly, and short-lived jobs; struggle to make child-care payments or tend to drug-addicted and imprisoned relatives. If they seek government assistance, there will be little or none, aside from the military. They may not even be able to apply for financial aid for school if their family's black-market livelihoods mean that their parents file no taxes. If they somehow do finally make it to any urban area for work, they may be more likely to be hired for entry-level positions or less likely to be shot in the street, but the cultural and educational gap will neutralize most other advantages. They will also quickly contrast their own plight with that of the city's other poor residents, noting what appear to be a wealth of resources provided via government aid programs and non-profits for everyone but them. In some places, they will see overseas immigrants—particularly resettled refugees—being given free housing and job training. In others, they will see non-profits offering free classes in financial planning, or help for students applying for financial aid, but all targeted toward "people of color"—one of those strange liberal shibboleths that seems almost designed to trick the ignorant into saying "colored people" in order to give better-off urbanites a proper target for class hatred thinly disguised as self-righteous scorn.

It's important to remember that the perception of such inequities certainly exceeds their reality, but they are not entirely imaginary. A rural migrant from McDowell County, West Virginia, is essentially an internal refugee, fleeing a majority white county that has a premature death rate (861.2 per 100,000 population) exceeded only by that of the notoriously poor Pine Ridge reservation.[44] But there are not only no substantial welfare programs targeting these parts of the country, there are also no NGOS or resettlement agencies waiting to aid these refugees when they escape such devastation. The irony is, of course, that the white rural migrant has far more in common with his Mexican, East African, or Middle Eastern counterpart than with the urban professional.[45] But this commonality is obscured from both ends: by racial resentment and Islamophobia stoked among the poor and by the Identitarian politics of privilege promoted by wealthier urbanites.

Since whites compose the bulk of the impoverished population, if not always its lowest rungs, the far left's persistent refusal to

address white poverty is a refusal to address the conditions of
the single largest demographic composing the lower class in the
United States—and one that has very clearly experienced the
J-Curve of heightened expectations suddenly plummeting into
a sharp reversal of prospects.[46] This is an inherently politicizing
process, and at this point the far right has been almost the only
force attempting to shape it. They tend to target the perceived
inequities pointed out above, combining xenophobia with a
very simple economic calculus. The Idaho Three Percenters, for
example, argue that the state ought not waste so many resources
resettling refugees when it is already doing such a poor job of
helping its own impoverished citizens. This is the gateway
argument for their entire program of localist Islamophobia,
which reaches its natural conclusion when they propose a
world of bearded, rifle-toting patriarchs defending their
respective compounds in the Rocky Mountains.

There are a few simple lessons that might be drawn from all
of this. The first overarching observation is simply that the
future of class war in the United States is beginning to enter
a period of severe polarization and extreme contingency. More
and more people are becoming aware that liberalism is a failed
political project. The ability of partisans to succeed in the environment of competitive control opened up by this failure will
correlate to their ability to offer strength and stability to populations in the midst of crisis. Many of these openings are appearing
first in the far hinterland, where the transposition of class antagonism onto racial divides in income, imprisonment, and mortality
is reaching a saturation point—the very intensity of long-term
economic crisis producing a commensurate crisis in the process
of racialization itself. But while organizing among poor whites is
a persistent necessity of any future revolutionary prospect, the far
hinterland does not provide a solid foundation for such activity,
due to its low share of total population, crumbling infrastructure,
and distance from key flows within the global economy. Any

attempt to organize in such conditions is quickly transformed into a quasi-communitarian attempt at local self-reliance— the endless repetition of those failed downriver communes, which invariably become retreats for urban Buddhists or walled compounds flying money-colored flags.

It should not in any way be remarkable that the far right has built some marginal support amongst rural whites, then. What *is* remarkable is the fact that their support among the rural poor has thus far been so marginal. Similarly, Trump was catapulted into the presidency not by resounding support among poor ruralites but instead by a massive wave of non-participation, as neither party had anything to offer. If white ruralites were as inherently conservative as the average leftist would have us believe, they should be flooding into far-right organizations in unprecedented numbers, demanding a platform for their racial resentment. But the reality is that, whether left wing or right wing, political activity is something that is built, not something that emerges naturally from the experience of oppression—this experience only places the success of political organization along a probabilistic curve and colors the character of its result. The far right has only been capable of attracting newcomers in rural areas in a spare few locations. Much of their apparent support base comes either from historical strongholds—such as the KKK counties of the South and those areas of Idaho, Montana, and Washington where white supremacists relocated in the 1990s—or from whitening exurbs, which have acted as a sort of geographical catchment for racial resentment in the United States and have recently begun to reach the limit of their urban tether. Maybe more importantly, in order to attract new recruits, the far right has had to tone down its explicit racism and foreground economics. But even this has been met mostly with apathy and wariness. The white population of the far hinterland still seems to find more promise in opiates than politics.

Kindness

One of the first times I remember camping along the Klamath was with my father and brother along a stretch of beach just past Weitchpec, a town of no more than five or six buildings over-looking the last merger of the major rivers before the Klamath spills into the sea. While my family was fishing downstream, I sat under a ragged blue tarp we'd strung between a few driftwood poles and the bed of our old F-150 4x4, its body so dented it was difficult to find a single stretch of smooth metal or unchipped paint on any of its surfaces. The entire thing was like a raised relief map of the area itself: snow-pale painted ridges giving way to complex folds of rust and dripping dew, a knot of steel mirroring the knot of wood and stone from which the machine had received its many scars—hauling timber for our trailer's fireplace, pulling stumps and stones to clear our gardens, and of course the innumerable times that truck bed had carried me, my brother, our cousins, and many other kin if not by blood then at least by mountain life. I was maybe fourteen at the time. I looked up through the tears in the blue tarp to the deeper blue of summer sky beyond, and then to the dim outline of the sun behind the plastic, burning into my eyes with a dull, persistent light. I closed my eyes, and that sun was still there, scorched into my eyelids in the shape of a white circle, slowly tumbling. When I opened them again, I looked toward the cool shadows crossing that wide river, fat from all the other rivers poured into it. I watched the opposite shore where a family of black bears had been playing earlier, shaking the underbrush and splashing in the shallows.

Soon another truck drove down from the main road, parking nearby. Two men got out, talking between each other in a language I didn't know. I waved and they waved back, yelling over in English, "Don't worry, if we'd wanted to shoot you, we would've done it from the truck!" It was marginally disconcerting, but also reassuring, since the logic was sound. You could probably murder someone here and get away with it even if you weren't really trying that hard. The body wouldn't be found for weeks, months, maybe never. Maybe it would be picked at by bears and coyotes and wild boars, melted to dust by swarms of insects, eaten by the river until nothing was left. Out here you could be utterly annihilated, your life gutted out of you until whatever you once were was reduced to a traceless waste, primal ooze sinking into water-smoothed stones and knotted roots. Life here seems to twist seamlessly into death. It's not just the river and forest that appear upside down, then, but every feature of time and geography. The sea reaches up into the mountains through salmon spawns, hordes of glittering fish charging up clogged waterways, their flesh red, rotting from their bodies as every ounce of muscle and fat is burned to throw them headlong into that final, semelparous orgy of eggs and corpses. Their nitrogen-rich bodies fill the bellies of martens, eagles, and bears, ocean-born nutrients ultimately built into the shape of a forest.[47] The inversion of land and sea also appears to turn time upside down, as giant armored sturgeons are pulled from the thalweg like primordial sea monsters.

Driving along the backward river, it often seems as though the ancient, green-clear water actually travels back in time, its ripples disappearing toward that ever-vanishing Eternal Now worshipped by the white baby boomer Buddhists in their southern Oregon temples. But rather than Buddha, we have Sasquatch, the giant's grim, furry body a neonate symbol of our own evolution. Like Santa Muerte, Sasquatch is simultaneously a death god and the atheistic icon of a deeply material apocalypse—one that first saw this land washed in the blood of genocide, its very essence chewed apart in mines and mills and, as if this were not enough, a second apocalypse then returning for the conquerors, their new life of work and wages torn from under them, poisons cast into their blood, the abandoned mines tainting the water and the culled forests unsettling the earth, causing landslides and feeding fuel into the ever-growing seasons of drought and flame.

Sasquatch watches over all of this, indifferent, a symbol of time disjointed, evolution running backwards. In those Chinese mountain temples, maybe some had prayed to a similar deity, that Monkey King who wiped his name from the ledgers of reincarnation and single-handedly smashed the armies of heaven—maybe not a coincidence, as they themselves were fleeing a civil war led by a commander who sought to destroy the imperial heaven of the Qing and replace it with a kingdom of peasants. But Sasquatch is not a god you can pray to, exactly. It is just a witness, a shadow of ourselves outside of time, watching. At night along the river roads, each curve is enveloped in a startling blackness, tree limbs dipping down like lampreys. You pass sleeping hamlets and abandoned houses, the river below winding along its own black path. The starlight stretches across its ripples like fragile sinews. And out of the darkness you will see the statues appear gradually—the metal sculpture of Sasquatch in Happy Camp, the many icons of burl and hardwood—all rising from the darkness like pale corpses being lifted out of tar. Everything takes shape except for the eyes, which remain oil-black, as if those unemployed sawyers had gouged the sockets all the way through to some other, subterranean reality. Those eyes watch you pass—not judging, not pleading, not proclaiming new laws or founding new heavens beneath the fir and spruce. Sasquatch can't free us. We can't be saved or born again.

The two men who had stopped by our campsite asked a series of questions to figure out where I was from and whom we might know in common—the customs that compose order in most territories that exist marginally beyond the law. My uncle worked a few construction sites in Happy Camp and Orleans—they vaguely knew the name. Afterwards they offered me some salmon, because they had too much, and invited me and my family to their Labor Day party down the beach. These small kindnesses are what remain when every other guarantee recedes. They pointed up the river, and I could see the distant, sun-blurred shapes of people moving there at the very horizon where stone met light—people approaching, maybe, or all of us sliding slowly toward them as if it were really the earth that moved and not the river, as if history were one gargantuan slide of soil, flesh, and shattered granite, massive enough that buried in its midst we see nothing but mud, blood, and bodies drowning in the lightless pressure. And yet nonetheless it is a flood of which we are a part, inhuman and human at once. You surface for a moment and through the dirt you can see that hatchet-edged horizon, the warm bodies moving freely in the light.

three

The Iron City

The crisis, nominally, was the crisis of '08 or '09. For those of us entering the labor force, though, it wasn't containable within a year, nor a span of them. Time couldn't keep it in because it seemed to change time—not only to devastate the simple economic time of fiscal quarters and recession years but to tear into the flesh of economics itself, digging under the upward-trending charts of profitability, global development, and the "information economy" to reach, finally, the hard, blood-soaked bone of that other, longer crisis that seemed now both to pre-date and to outlive our collapsing economy altogether.

The crisis became indescribably intimate. It defined us: a generational crisis, certainly, but also something more. Something that threw us backward to the inauguration of the long downswing in profitability that began in the late 1960s or early '70s and at the same time linked us forward to the fires on the horizon, as it became clear that we were not a single, temporarily fucked generation but instead the first in a grand parade of the futureless. It was inside of us somehow, defining our decisions, shaping our bodies, tearing our relationships up at the root. And it was in the landscape as well. After my seasonal contract in Nevada ran out in the fall of 2011, I drove south to Los Angeles in a dust-caked Chevy Metro with brake-pads that had been ground down to the metal. Housing developments stood ponderous in the golden dust of California's deserts, the frames gutted by suburban miners looking to sell the wiring for scrap. I slept in my car and talked to the many newly homeless. They said the same things, mostly, because they'd lost everything in more or less the same way, the same crisis. They said I should have stayed in Nevada—that I should have bought a gun there when I had the chance because out here the police will kill you for nothing so you might as well shoot back.

There was no work in California so I drove north, trying to get as far as I could before the brakes gave out entirely. The wildfires had started late that year and the early autumn air was smoke-gray from the clouds down to the rattling, yellowed grass—an ecological crisis to accompany the economic, all rolling over us in slow waves of ash-choked, ambient doom. The smoke blurred the shapes around you, people's silhouettes bleeding into each other, the mountains and forests looming through it like occulted gods. And the worst part wasn't that it stung your eyes and burned when you breathed but that you realized how easy it became to live with it. This was the next world, the "new normal" as they had begun to say, and we could, unfortunately, survive.

By the time I reached Seattle, the smoke had cleared. At first it seemed as if a different climate somehow governed this city, encircled by a bubble of clean air and moderate economic prosperity. Skyscrapers and construction cranes glinted in the late-setting September sun. Staring at the skyline, you could almost hear the capital pouring in from the other end of the Pacific Rim, still inflated by the Chinese stimulus. It was my first time attempting to live in such a city—in any city, really. People often don't realize that the barriers to entry for these narrow corridors of prosperity are almost impossibly high for those of us migrating from the countryside. It's easy enough to find some shitty vehicle and drive out to settle in another part of the low-wage, low-rent outer hinterland, but without friends, relatives, or the fraternity of some criminal network in an urban area, you get caught in a loop of seasonal work and unemployment, never quite able to save up enough for gas to make it to the city, or first, last, and deposit to rent someplace until you find work. Without an address, you don't get the job. Without the job, no landlord will rent to you.

Even here, then, that skyline remained distant. For the first week, I stayed in SeaTac, an airport suburb south of the city. Across the street from my motel, there was a graveyard laid out on the last plot before the landing strips began. Every few minutes, planes would dip down low enough to shake the coffins. For dinner, I'd walk north along International Boulevard to eat goat gyros at a halal grocery store or cheap cheeseburgers at a 1950s-style diner filled with white retirees left over from the suburb's heyday. If you kept walking north, you'd reach Tukwila, an old Boeing suburb now split between industrial districts, the largest shopping mall in the Northwest, and housing complexes filled with migrant workers. Past a strip club, a mosque, and a trailer park, the Boulevard turns and pitches downward into the Duwamish River valley, filled with factories, casinos, and Superfund hazard sites. At the point where the road curves and changes grade, you can stand in the parking lot of an abandoned gas station emblazoned with No Trespassing signs and see below the entire industrial stretch leading up to the port and, behind it, the far-off city glittering in the night. Just behind the blind curve, however, stand the reflective-glass offices of the Department of Homeland Security, peering over the same expanse like a gatekeeper.

It was one of those things that I would remember even after moving up to that shining city, renting slivers of rooms backlit at night by the glow of those glittering buildings and working for minimum wage in a wholesale kitchen lost somewhere in that southward industrial expanse, making pre-packaged salads and sandwiches to be sold in those towers now physically nearer but still in every way so distant—a reminder that this city was not mine, that it would never be, save for maybe the few months we camped in its central plaza before Occupy Seattle died out in a wave of slowly receding riots. Even as the shattered windows of the business district showered us in their glittering light, I remembered that well-guarded vista, the nights in that southern suburb peppered with the sound of doors being kicked in—sometimes by ICE, sometimes by SWAT, sometimes by soldiers from who knows what authority. Those same powers, really, that would round us up after the riots, applying criminal charges in a seemingly random fashion just to prove that "order" had been restored.

It was only in those dull chrome holding cells and glass-glittering streets that I fully realized how cold that distant landscape had been, the downtown towers simply the crystallization of dead labor drawn together from all across the globe, the streets nothing but corridors for cops and capital. Everything that we were doing there—rioting, occupying, walking out of our jobs as fast-food workers—was all caught up already in the spectacle of itself, captured in a cold, dead space built to contain it. And it was really only from outside the walls that this could be seen clearly. That hinterland of decaying, industrialized suburbia seemed to offer a certain counterpoint to the "creative class" and its urban palace. From this distance, hidden sightlines could be found and the occluded core of the region's economy unveiled.

Logistics Cities

Seattle has always been a gateway. Beginning as little more than a bayside milling town in a timber supply chain, its first industrial structure facilitated the extraction of natural resources out of the rural hinterland of the Pacific Northwest. Soon this early infrastructure was repurposed as the supply chain shifted northward, the city becoming a key node in the transit of commodities and labor between the Klondike gold fields and the continental

United States.[1] During the world wars, the city's physical geography and pre-existing role in important supply chains secured its future as a major military-industrial hub, anchored by Boeing. During the Cold War, this military influence extended into the service sector, CIA and other defense funds ballooning the University of Washington into one of the region's largest employers. But, as production in the U.S. and Europe began to hit the limits of profitability in the late 1960s, the firms that did not go bankrupt began to build new international supply chains in order to access cheaper pools of labor overseas. This process would not have been possible without the ability to coordinate an incredibly complex global network producing and circulating an unprecedented volume of goods. New digital technologies were combined with wartime management practices and engineering advances in shipping (such as containerization and the scaling-up of air and sea freight systems) in a global logistics revolution that made previously unimaginable, world-spanning supply chains a reality.[2]

Cities like Seattle were well positioned to benefit from these changes. The official story of the city's "postindustrial" reinvention is that the industrial Seattle of the past was rescued from its collapse by Microsoft in the first tech boom in the 1990s. This was followed by an influx of "creatives" and accompanying build-up of the FIRE industries and other producer services throughout the first decades of the twenty-first century. In reality, though, Seattle's revival is in large part due simply to its location along important chokepoints in global supply chains, paired with its wealth of resources in heavy industry and its military heritage. The ascent of China—a near neighbor by air and water, due to the city's latitude—ensured a stable position for the metro area's ports and shipping industry in the new global order. This was clear as early as 1979, a year in which Seattle saw both the founding of global logistics giant Expeditors International and received Deng Xiaoping on his first tour of the U.S. Deng spoke at the

Boeing factory in Everett—an event that would be repeated by Xi Jinping in his own tour of the United States in 2015. In the years following Deng's visit, a series of trade deals were signed with the port authority, laying the groundwork for Washington State to become the largest exporter (in dollar value) of China-bound goods.[3]

But this is not simply a curiosity of geopolitics. With the global landscape of production and management increasingly concentrated in a handful of mega-urban agglomerations per continent, the simple movement of goods becomes a massive technical hurdle. Though it may seem at first as if these metropolitan cores are themselves the center of the global economy, they are more accurately the tip of an economic iceberg. The rural spaces of the far hinterland explored above are the deepest sunken edges of this iceberg, but its real bulk lies somewhere between those black depths and the shining white seracs of the urban skyline. The true center of the world economy is not to be found in the "creative," financialized, or high-tech downtown cores of its global cities, but instead in the complex mesh of material infrastructure that links them together. The geography of the long crisis is therefore one of small green zones nested in vast logistics-industrial spaces that extend laterally from these cores, dwindling finally to rural spaces crosscut by thin transit corridors.

So below Seattle the "global city," there still exists that second, older metropolis: the logistics city, now exploded into a network of industrial lowlands. Even though services tend to dominate the metro's overall employment profile, jobs in manufacturing, wholesale trade, warehousing, and transportation tend to cluster around the seaports, airports, and rail yards in South King County and North Pierce County, all linked to one another by similarly high employment shares along transit corridors. There are four primary hubs,[4] in which manufacturing as a share of total employment in individual Census tracts gets as high as 46 percent, and most tracts have somewhere between two and five times as much employment in manufacturing as the metro area as a whole. Similarly, the same areas see their share of non-manufacturing logistics employment reach a high of 53 percent, most tracts having between two and seven times as much employment in non-manufacturing logistics as the greater metro area.[5]

Even where this near hinterland has retained a modicum of its older productive character—as with aeronautics in the Seattle suburbs—this production itself is now linked to the global economy in a wholly different way. As Jasper Bernes notes in his seminal article on the topic,

> In the idealised world-picture of logistics, manufacture is merely one moment in a continuous, Heraclitean flux; the factory dissolves into planetary flows, chopped up into modular, component processes which, separated by thousands of miles, combine and recombine according to the changing whims of capital.[6]

This ideal is never realized, of course, but it is the vanishing-point toward which these logistics spaces strive. And because of this, they have their own logics of aggregation and extension, distinct from those seen in the service sector cores.

Logistical functions tend to concentrate around interfaces between economies of different scale—usually where the local contacts the national or global economy. Such interfaces take the form of logistics nodes, as seen in the example of Seattle. Most often these are seaports, airports, or river ports, but also sometimes landlocked border crossings or other historically inherited hubs (as with the processing and warehousing industries in south Chicago, Illinois, an artifact of the national railway system's original structure). The spaces then expand laterally in corridors that follow major freight routes such as interstates, railroads, and rivers. Here containers, parcels, unpackaged commodities, and unfinished goods are sorted, processed, packaged, and transferred from one mode of transportation to the next. As these corridors extend farther from logistics hubs, they also tend to narrow out into thin transit strips with few stops between—the railroads and interstates cutting through rural areas are the obvious examples, though major rivers play much the same role, and the process approaches its own standard of perfection with the flight path.

At the most extreme, the combination of hubs and corridors making up a logistics space can grow to encompass large segments of entire cities, as is the case with the FedEx "Superhub" in Memphis, Tennessee, and the UPS "World Port" in Lexington, Kentucky.[7] In Memphis, for example, FedEx alone employed some 30,000 people in 2015,[8] which was nearly 5 percent of the city's total population, while manufacturing, wholesale trade, and transportation and warehousing collectively accounted for almost a quarter of all employment in the metropolitan area in 2014 (a third if waste management and remediation is also included).[9] Nor do these numbers necessarily cover employment at companies like Walmart, which is often counted as simply a retailer, rather than a logistics company, despite its massive warehouses and e-commerce wing. Since there are no clear-cut variables for "logistics" as such in U.S. industrial statistics, such numbers capture the phenomenon in a second-hand way, but the trend is still apparent.

In general, urban logistics spaces today tend to cluster along cities' outer fringes and inner ring suburbs. In many cases, the location of a major port or other hub may be located near the downtown core, but the industrial zones that accompany it will tend to spread away from the core as best as possible. These activities require large amounts of space, since they tend to distribute horizontally along transit routes and require large, single-story warehouse-style buildings for ease of loading and unloading. With real estate speculation accompanying influxes of "creatives" and professionals to the urban core, industrial spaces left over from past incarnations of the inner city are rapidly converted into clubs, cafés, and CrossFit gyms for hip urbanites. It thus becomes far more affordable to purchase empty land or abandoned warehouses and big-box shopping centers on the urban outskirts.

This competition over land arises due to the increasing concentration of all economic activity into a few mega-urban agglomerations at both the global and national scale. Each post-recession "recovery" has seen both diminishing job creation rates and an increasing concentration of those dwindling jobs in just a handful of the most populous counties.[10] The result was that, between 2010 and 2014, 73 counties holding 34 percent of the total u.s. population received 50 percent of new jobs.[11] Overall, counties with 500,000 residents or more accounted for 81 percent of all new establishments created and 64 percent of all new jobs, while counties with fewer than 100,000 residents simply saw no growth whatsoever in establishments and accounted for only 9 percent of total job growth.[12] The logistics city and the global city are therefore simultaneously fused together and forced to compete for premium space in the same urban agglomerations. This industrial conflict drives urban development patterns and defines the class terrain of most major American cities today.

Atmospheres

Seattle is constrained by geology, squeezed between water bodies and constructed along natural sightlines. The glacial history of the region created a landscape in which drumlin ridges run north–south, separated by deep valleys, all artifacts of an ancient climatic shift that devastated the hemisphere and reshaped the very face of the earth. Today, however, it is a climate refuge zone—one of the few parts of the world where the effects of global warming will remain mild in the immediate future.[13] This also means that it's expected to become a sort of catchment for environmental refugees fleeing the destabilizing effects of climate change worldwide. In a certain sense, this is already visible, as new migrants have flooded into the area in the past two decades from all parts of the world, but particularly from areas (such as East Africa and Southeast Asia) already feeling the effects of drought and rising sea levels. Overall, the foreign-born population grew five times faster than the native-born population between 2000 and 2014, composing roughly 21 percent of the total county population.[14]

My years spent living in the urban core as a food service worker were marked by a series of protests, occupations, riots, and strikes, beginning in 2011 with my involvement in Occupy Seattle and capped in 2014 by several months of incarceration in the county work-release unit on charges related to a riot in 2012. The work-release unit was itself a sort of microcosm of the new Seattle that existed beyond the "revitalized" core. It was organized into a dorm system, with two beds to a cell and twenty or so cells to a dorm, and in it I was living in close quarters with a good demographic cross-section of the city's poorer districts. The story told by these dorms was one in which out-migration from the urban core and new migrant settlement at the city's edges has created a demographic shift in the nature of the Seattle area's segregation. Rather than dividing into majority-white, majority-black, majority-Asian, or majority-Hispanic neighborhoods, the city is segregated roughly into high-income, low-to-moderate-diversity areas in the north and low-income, hyper-diverse areas in the south.[15] Most other prisoners were from the south end or the southern suburbs, with little racial sorting by neighborhood, though between one-third and one-half were foreign-born. This type of segregation is becoming the standard in many cities that have experienced economic booms and in-migration in the first decades of the twenty-first century.

Migration in the u.s. has followed jobs, essentially starting a new cycle of concentrated urbanization in an already heavily urbanized nation.[16] Some of the new migrants are working in the still-booming tech and cultural industries of the urban core, but job growth overall has been in low-wage sectors.[17] This bifurcates not only the employment profiles of these cities, but their geography. As higher-paid arrivals flood the urban core, rising rents force poorer residents out to the city's edges and into increasingly impoverished inner ring suburbs. This same dynamic also ensures that new migrants working low-wage jobs will settle in the same areas. In Seattle's southern suburbs, the industrial lowlands are therefore hemmed by ridge-top settlements with higher poverty rates, lower incomes, smaller white populations, and larger shares of foreign-born. This is where many of those employed in the region's logistics and manufacturing industries actually live.[18]

Only focusing on the gentrification of the urban core often doesn't capture the entirety of this dynamic, which political scientist Alan Ehrenhalt calls "the great inversion." In this process, the development of the urban core drives a reversal of the postwar norm, in which poverty clustered in the inner city and wealth in the suburbs. Now the inner city tends to house those with higher incomes, and those with higher incomes tend to be whiter. Meanwhile, suburbia becomes fiercely polarized: "In 1960, the average income gap between America's richest and poorest inner suburbs was about 2.1 to 1. Now it is about 3.4 to 1."[19] The upper-end suburbs might house tech workers in new developments adjacent to green-fielded corporate campuses, as in Kirkland and Redmond in the Seattle area, but at the opposite end are the inner-ring suburbs populated by those at the bottom of the employment hierarchy:

> They tend to house a transient population, nearly all of it composed of minorities, and possess a housing stock dominated by apartment buildings, many of whose tenants left now-demolished high-rise public housing within the inner city.[20]

Some suburbs still exist somewhere in between these two poles, but most seem to be dropping, rather than rising, as the middle slowly erodes.[21] Overall, the years after the last crisis saw poverty grow to record levels (an average of around 45 million people living under the poverty line),[22] and over the last decade and a half suburban poverty has grown at almost twice the rate as its urban counterpart. As early as 2011, the suburbs housed more poor than the cities—with 16.4 million suburban poor making up about one-third of the national total.[23]

The result is that many old postwar suburbs that once hosted the better paid, predominantly white segments of the workforce are converted into new, hyperdiverse proletarian neighborhoods. These neighborhoods intersect with the logistics spaces located in this same urban fringe, such that day-to-day life in the near hinterland is shaped by the infrastructure of the global economy in a direct way not experienced in the central city. Driving from one place to another means navigating airport freight roads, weaving through mazes of cargo trucks, winding across labyrinths of warehouses and factories. These are spaces built at the scale of capital, rather than people. There is no hipster nostalgia for "walkability" here—many suburbs even lack complete sidewalk systems—and going anywhere is synonymous with driving there. This creates a different atmosphere of life, changing the way your body seems to move through space, to inhabit these decaying, lead-painted postwar houses, once the epitome of middling affluence. Different segments of the population can thus have fundamentally different impressions of life within what is nominally the same metropolis.

Algorithms

Located in the attic at the top of the King County Courthouse in downtown Seattle, one consolation offered by the work-release unit was the view. From our dorm, we had panoramic windows (with bars to prevent suicide) opening onto the southern stretch of the city, including the stadiums, the port, and the Sodo industrial area. The natural sightline of the glacial valley ensured that on clear days you could see all the way down the stretch of railroads, factories, and warehouses to where the planes descend onto Boeing Field, the region's primary freight airport. The landscape is one of catastrophes layered atop one another. As you travel south the people get poorer, the work gets harder, the air, soil, and water get dirtier and everything begins to feel far more faceless. People are atomized into old housing complexes and decaying postwar, single-family homes scattered between vast, almost-incomprehensible infrastructures designed not for human habitation but instead for the efficient circulation of goods. There is no communal space. Instead, there are only small, exploded cores of retail and leisure, where human interaction is reduced to the buying and selling of things.

But this doesn't really become apparent until day-to-day life begins to break down. In work-release, technically an "alternative to confinement," you're allowed to leave the building if you have a job or school to attend, so long as you can have all your time outside accounted for by supervisors. If you have unaccounted-for time, you're sent back to the county jail. If you're late, you are sent to back to county. If you're caught doing things other than working or looking for work, you're sent back to county. Your work "privileges" can be revoked by your caseworker at any time, so there's always a chance that you simply won't be able to make it out and may lose your job for it. Some employers actually preferred these terms, since it meant that their workers had little leeway to agitate for higher wages or workplace protections. Several of the recycling centers in Sodo recruited from the work-release unit directly, hiring the prisoners to sort the unwashed and often-dangerous recyclables.

Though ostensibly run by the resident caseworkers, the entire system was actually dependent on an underlying software system.

It was this software system that had the ultimate authority, since it was the reference used by the guards to let you out to work or to record when you should be back. There were stories, of course. Sometimes the caseworker had input the data incorrectly and you weren't allowed out for the day. Even worse was if they had input the wrong return time, meaning that people would be sent back to county upon their return (and maybe charged with a felony for "escaping") simply because the computer system said they should have been back hours before and the caseworkers had left for the weekend. Those who had been living in the unit for the longest told stories about people who'd been sent to county on a computer error and ended up serving the rest of their sentence there and losing their jobs, since the caseworker took three weeks to receive and process their complaint.

One day, the entire system simply crashed. No one could be let out because when the software rebooted, all the data had been erased. The "alternative" to confinement became a little less alternative, as over a hundred prisoner-workers were stuck inside dorms that weren't really designed for full capacity. The caseworkers called people up one by one to re-input the schedules, which had to be confirmed again each time with everybody's supervisors at work. The crash happened on a Thursday, and many of us didn't have our schedules input again until the following Monday. The worst thing wasn't really the wages lost or being stuck inside; it was just that the entire illusion had collapsed for a moment and, when it did, the other, ancillary illusions also briefly flickered off. It wasn't that we had to reckon with the fact that we were imprisoned, but instead with the fact that work wasn't really an escape. We sat around playing hearts and talking about what we used to do before we were in and what we would do when we were out, even when we knew the reality was that we had done and would be doing much the same thing, only more alone. When things break, it only shows that everything is already broken.

That industrial stretch beyond the windows was not freedom in any real sense of the word. It was just a long catastrophe, abutted by neighborhoods filled with people fleeing other catastrophes, some rapid, some excruciatingly slow. We move from one to the other convincing ourselves that we have somehow escaped. Workers come down from the jails and housing complexes to staff the recycling centers or the vast, alien warehouses where their every action will be guided by the incomprehensible command of some software system compiling stock for just-in-time delivery, those warehouses themselves built in glacier-cut valleys now a floodplain for polluted rivers eroding down into lahar deposits—strata left from the last volcanic eruption, when Rainier had spewed out rolling clouds of magma-infused mud and scalding vapor, incinerating the lowlands in a hurricane of ash. It's the same land where the squatter settlements had been built in the Great Depression, before the Navy burned them to the ground. Economic catastrophe layered on natural disaster, and now natural disaster dictated by economic demand.

But when things break, we are also given the chance to forge something communal out of the ruins. After several of us got out, we met up a few times at the casino. Playing cards now had a certain comfort to it, and the urge to gamble was almost irresistible after having every modicum of our lives governed in so much detail by inscrutable algorithms. The casino was in Tukwila—a squat, glowing building on a triangle of land sitting between the railroad, the highway, and Boeing Field. Outside, semi-trucks hurled past, heavy with packages heading out to the warehouses, or maybe barren, ratchet straps rattling against the empty beds as they slowed before the airstrip. Different details governed by different algorithms. Left with nothing else, we could at least enjoy the momentary freedom that accompanied sheer chance, even if the odds weren't in our favor. The casino was filled with others like us, people trying desperately to break the idiotic monotony of work and wages. It didn't matter if they lost. One of my friends—a tall Taiwanese man whom I'd practice my mandarin with in the hallway between cells—confessed that he felt lonely now that he was out. Inside, he'd had more friends than he'd ever had, he said. Now he just went from his apartment to his job and back again. He sold cell phones for forty waking hours each week. At home, he'd watch Netflix. Sometimes an entire day would go by in which he'd talk to no one except for his supervisor and a few customers. Maybe when everyone was out, we could all get together again and go to Vegas, he'd suggested. Or maybe Reno—anywhere we could make bigger bets.

Inversion

In 2008, before living in Seattle, Nevada, or overseas, I had moved from rural California to rural Wisconsin to finish a four-year degree after a couple years spent in the community college system. I studied something frivolous on a low-income scholarship, worked the night audit at a local Super 8 Motel, and traveled around the ruins of the rural Midwest in my time off. The area that I lived in was filled with long-abandoned settlements, overgrown farms, and towering industrial ruins. The most notable of these were the ore docks and other remnants of port facilities along Lake Superior. These docks were vast skeletons of steel and wood, with abandoned railroads arcing up hundreds of feet in the air to meet fleets of long-sunken ships carrying cargoes of timber and ore drawn from the north woods to build the cities of America's early industrial boom.

Today, only ruin industries remain. Some of the most lucrative logging is done by divers in Lake Superior who haul up the old growth dropped from ships more than a hundred years ago. Small-scale farmers cut out new market niches with organic crops and dairy products, imagining a "green future," despite low productivity and high prices. Mines return to the region with new, more ruthless techniques to be used in the absence of ore veins. The rock is melted down and minerals harvested through a complex process of chemical distillation, the effluence dumped in nearby "containment" sites patrolled by paramilitaries. Some of the old docks have even been retained, as in Marquette, Michigan, where the new mines can easily unload their smaller but more valuable payloads. Elsewhere, tourism or energy production dominate the employment profile, common features of areas largely left behind by today's industrial agglomeration.

Economic activity is largely concentrated according to arbitrary factors of history and geography. In most cases, the whims of a handful of billionaires have combined with historically inherited geographical or infrastructural endowments to define the upwardly mobile cities of the twenty-first century. While city governments across the country shower money on snake oil consultants who promise to unlock the secrets of attracting hip, creative millennials to even the most unattractive of cities, the fact remains that most places simply do not have the necessary characteristics to become the next Austin, Texas, or Atlanta, Georgia. This is especially true given the fact that they are competing for a shrinking pool of capital that, when invested in high-tech industries, produces a remarkably low number of jobs, despite the multiplier effect. If a city does not have a major seaport (like most of the coastal metropoles); a geographically important location, often combined with major railroad or highway hub (Chicago; Indianapolis, Indiana; Denver, Colorado); or a government or military cluster (Washington, DC; San Diego, California; Colorado Springs, Colorado), then the competition grows far more extreme.

Historical inheritance plays a large role as well, especially in "brain hubs" around university complexes. This is visible in Silicon Valley's connection with Stanford, the Boston area's dependence on the education industry and related research and development, and the Raleigh-Durham-Chapel Hill Research Triangle in North Carolina. Many smaller cities also follow this pattern, essentially acting as one-industry college towns riding the student debt bubble as long as they can. Others centralize around small clusters of insurance and healthcare hubs, surfing a similar bubble. This small-town dimension of the American hinterland is one staffed by administrative workers of all sorts, essentially bureaucrats stuffed into the bloated body of state-backed speculative schemes in the sorely inefficient healthcare and education sectors. Any attempt to rationalize or equitably reform these industries will also, in effect, threaten the livelihoods of these corners of the hinterland, which still often conceive of themselves as vaguely middle class. These small-to-medium towns with mid-range service economies would almost certainly be the first to be sacrificed if the bubbles collapse or if meaningful student debt and healthcare reforms were put into motion.

Other cities seem to be little more than a sequence of economic booms, the first of which were essentially random, though the success of one also tended to make future success more probable. Often the historical boom of one industry can concentrate capital, which then allows for further investment and diversification outside the original boom industry—this is the case with the major oil cities of Texas, as well as with the more recent boom in North Dakota. Others have historical endowments simply due to their concentration of wealthy individuals or leisure activity, as is seen in Santa Fe, New Mexico; Las Vegas, Nevada; Connecticut's Gold Coast; or even significantly smaller, second-home leisure cities like Aspen, Colorado. These sorts of historical endowments tend to define concentration at the local and state levels, even if many of these cities may not play the same global role as New York or Silicon Valley. Often such cities (Wichita, Kansas; Iowa City, Iowa; Reno, Nevada) are dependent on a single, relatively small industrial complex, the loss of which would be capable of unbinding the entire local economy—as has already happened with many of the smaller Rust Belt cities of the northeast.

In Wisconsin, the harshest dissonance came not from the wreckage of the industrial past coexisting with myths of a new "green" economy to come, but instead from the age of this particular Rust Belt. This was not a region simply bankrupt by the post-1970s restructuring, like much of the northeast, nor was it just one among many areas passed over for wartime or New Deal investment during the twentieth-century's middle age of war and depression. Instead, these ore docks and sunken ships were the ruined pillars of an industrial edifice that began its collapse as soon as it was built, ultimately becoming little more than an ancillary to greater cities along the southern stretches of the Great Lakes. It was not just a Rust Belt, then, but a single ghostlike megacity that had never taken form. Stillborn, its remains were overgrown, often barely recognizable as things built by humans: pillars of finely designed iron, steel, and concrete now vine-wrapped, eroded, and regressed to their deeper geological natures.

The ore docks had followed the railroads, most built in the late nineteenth century and the last built around the First World War to supply renewed demand for steel in the industrial core. Early on, the region imagined that it would become an economic capital unto itself, comparable to Chicago in its industrial capacity and exceeding it in natural amenities. In 1893 the city of Ashland, Wisconsin, hosted sixteen commercial docks and loaded seven thousand ships, the second busiest port on the Great Lakes.[24] Population had exploded and receded several times, following the whims of the railroads and industrial crises that defined the later nineteenth century. At one point, the city had declined from a population of hundreds to just a single family who would cycle through different abandoned houses at their whim. When the railroad chose the area for its bayside terminus, however, the population recovered, and the town was deemed "The Future Iron City of Lake Superior." But the Panic of 1873—called the

Great Depression before it was superseded by greater ones—was followed by a series of labor conflicts, the peak of which was the "Ashland War" in the winter of 1872/3, in which workers demanding unpaid wages were rounded up by a local militia and forced to walk 80 miles to a neighboring town in the subzero winter. Another brief boom saw the construction of the first ore docks, offering a glimpse at the prophesied "Iron City"—a mirage that collapsed again with the Panic of 1893.[25] The next boom came in the early 1900s, followed by the Panic of 1907, the Panic of 1910–11, the recession of 1913–14, and the First World War boom that would see the last of the ore docks constructed, at which point there was little left in the old dream of the northern metropolis. Harsh winter blizzards passed over the industrial skeletons, guaranteed to be nothing more than servants to an economic renaissance centered elsewhere.

The different character of economic concentration today similarly leads to different intensities of logistics activity, as well as a nationally uneven distribution of the general trend toward demographic inversion, in which the urban core is gentrified and the suburbs impoverished. On one level, this can be understood regionally. Coastal cities have tended to perform best, since they are where all the factors for economic concentration tend to be combined—seaports, rail and interstate hubs, first-stop destinations for foreign air freight, and historical endowments in the form of established universities, wealthy residents, and leisure industries. The global character of the post-1970s economic restructuring has tended to benefit those cities that are best connected to international circuits for capital and commodities, while depriving those that are landlocked. Even where manufacturing had been an economic base for such coastal cities, its destruction has largely been complemented by an influx of new industries. These are the cities pointed to as the unparalleled success stories of the "information economy," which others attempt in vain to emulate.

In these coastal cities, the same pattern of demographic inversion visible in Seattle is the standard. The old inner-city slums are redeveloped; many of the original residents leave as an influx of wealthier, whiter residents drives simultaneous booms in private development and public investment in things like street cars, light rail systems, bike lanes, and public parks. On the urban fringes and in the inner-ring suburbs, those forced out of the core or leaving what remains of inner-city slums mix with new migrants—both poorer domestic migrants attracted by economic opportunity and the foreign-born. This creates a second sequence of "white flight," as predominantly white suburbs are converted into new ghettoes and immigrant gateways. Many of the younger white suburbanites may be attracted to the revitalized downtown, but just as many white residents in the outer city and inner suburbs have continued the historical pattern of outward migration, moving to ever further exurbs.

But there are other areas that take on the character seen in places like northern Wisconsin—once imagined to be a great industrial complex, now reduced to an essentially rural existence, defined by the characteristics observed in other parts of the far hinterland. In winter, when the lake froze, you could walk out on the ice and climb onto the only remaining ore dock, otherwise inaccessible. I went once with a friend as a blizzard gathered in the northern stretches of the jagged, iced-over wasteland that was Lake Superior. From the edge of the dock, you could see it coming like a giant wall of static. Ice fishermen gathered around their small portals of black water as if praying to the gods drowned there, hauling their lines before scattering in their chained-up pickups and snowmobiles. My friend was a former train hopper from the slum suburbs beyond Chicago, recalling to me knife fights between juggalos and tweaker gangs who liked to throw traveler kids off trains for fun. As the blizzard neared, the snow shot horizontally through the dock's towering concrete pillars, as if we were on some sort of entirely uncontrollable vessel traveling at a great speed towards a destination that we could neither see nor choose.

This feeling is what I tend to recall when trying to imagine the true scale of these massive, seemingly immovable economic trends. Within such things, the present appears irreducibly complex and the future inscrutable. This is as true in the upwardly mobile coastal metropoles as in the old, largely land-locked manufacturing regions—the only remaining places within the U.S. where the demographic inversion has not yet fully taken hold.[26] Detroit, Michigan; Cleveland, Ohio; Buffalo, New York; Baltimore, Maryland; St Louis, Missouri; and smaller cities like Scranton, Pennsylvania; Flint, Michigan; Akron, Ohio; and thousands of small- to medium-sized manufacturing towns across the Northeast have all seen massive job losses since the 1970s, usually accompanied by major population loss. In small towns, this can leave only a hollowed-out shell, as the young follow capital's flow to the core cities. In larger metropolitan areas, these trends have only deepened the poverty of what we have come to think of as the prototypical inner-city slum. Those who can leave, do. This began with white flight to the suburbs and beyond, expanding the hollow core of the city into ever-poorer inner-ring suburbs encircled by ever-farther white exurbs. It reaches a certain completion with general out-migration from both city and suburbs to more successful urban areas, threatening a ruralization comparable to that seen in the ruins of the "Iron City" to the north.

But just as gentrification alone fails accurately to characterize the entirety of the demographic inversion elsewhere, white flight is a completely insufficient account of population loss in many Rust Belt cities. Most stages of this process also include a large-scale migration of the wealthier, better-educated black population. Some within the black middle and lower-middle class leave the problems of the inner-city slum, seeking better schools and services in the nearest suburbs. But this is only accompanied by further white flight (and the drying-up of tax dollars) in these suburbs, which tend to become little more than new branches of the ever-widening economic blight. Many of the better educated within the black upper-middle class are therefore traveling further, often returning to the Southern states from which their families migrated in the mid-twentieth century in a new population flow that some demographers have characterized as the Third Great Migration.[27]

Only the poorest remain in these central cities of the Rust Belt. This produces a seemingly paradoxical situation in which segregation increases at the same time that urban areas in general have become more diverse. In some cities, both dynamics are at play—this is particularly true in the eastern coastal cities, which have inherited the benefits of seaports and high finance, while also being essentially contiguous with the northeastern Rust Belt. In many cases, development of the downtown core has simply displaced zones of segregation further out into the suburbs, meaning that "many cities are seeing an increase in integrated neighborhoods *and* an increase in segregated ones at the same time."[28] In Chicago, for example, "the black population declined by 177,401" and "many went to suburbs surrounding the city on all sides, including suburbs many miles distant from the city limits," resulting in an overall pattern in which "between 2000 and 2010, Chicago became a whiter city with a larger affluent population."[29]

But most Rust Belt cities failed to follow suit. Instead, the hollowing-out of the urban core in such cities has made them resemble more and more the rural spaces of the far hinterland described in earlier chapters. In inner-city Detroit, "between 1978 and 1998, the city issued 9,000 building permits for new homes and 108,000 demolition permits, and quite a lot of structures were annihilated without official sanction."[30] And in 2010, justified as an attempt to concentrate population to provide better services and rid the city of blight, the mayor's office began a campaign to demolish a further quarter of the city's buildings.[31]

Unemployment rates of "somewhere around 40 to 50 percent"[32] mirror the rates found in zones of deep rural poverty. Similarly, much of the existing economy is informal and often illegal.

The main difference between the Rust Belt's inner cities and the far corners of rural America is simply the fact that they are still adjacent to relatively affluent, if shrinking, zones of accumulation. These more affluent areas take the form of both the cloistered downtown core and of remnant "traditional" suburbs, as in predominantly white suburban Baltimore County. In cities like Detroit, the mass demolition is only part of an attempt to revive the city's downtown—the hope being that development can follow demolition in the many new greenfield sites opened by the program. In some cases, as in Detroit, St Louis, and Baltimore, the revitalized downtown has remained relatively small and constrained. In others, such as Pittsburgh and Philadelphia, Pennsylvania, the revitalized zone is growing faster, but there is little to no buffer between it and the hollow core of slums beyond. And in some cities, such as Cleveland, Ohio, it seems as if downtown is simply refusing to be revitalized.

The future of these areas is hard to determine, but it could well be a properly rural decline in which new crises wipe out the shrinking zones of affluence one by one, like embers dying after the fire has burnt away. Though comparable to the collapse of that boreal "Iron City of Lake Superior," today this would require a rate of demolition befitting our era of gargantuan collapse. It would also entail the qualitatively different process of converting the properly urban into the rural, rather than a process in which a zone of rural subsistence fails to grow beyond the limits of a few medium-sized cities and small towns, despite population booms and high expectations. The results of future crises are likely to be just as gigantic and unpredictable, however. In Wisconsin, loud diesel Dodge trucks could often be seen roaring from one fishing hole to the next, all while flying their large Confederate flags within spitting distance of a lake that bordered Canada. Another friend who spent time in the local juvenile jail system for robbing a Taco John's told stories about how one prison guard with swastika tattoos would greet new Ojibwe inmates with initiatory beatings, just to make the hierarchy clear. At the same time, any nascent left wing was lost in a million minor subsistence projects, centered on a network of anarchist-ish organic farms and indigenous heritage groups. Another friend—that same train-hopper from the logistics cities of Chicago—had moved up to the area after hearing stories about how a particular sect of *midewinini* had gotten into gunfights with the FBI back in the 1970s. He had hoped that some of that momentum remained, only to find that those who weren't dead had mostly retired into NGOs, herding hopeful Teach For America white kids on and off the rez.

Sunbelts

The patterns observed in American cities, though distinct, are not exclusively American. There are many rust belts in the world, just as there are many "brain hubs." The latter, in particular, tend to be remarkably homogenous, with each financial district a hollow, gilded clone of those that came before and each hip neighborhood populated by clean sans-serif storefronts, exposed steel, and bare wood countertops, every now and then a dive bar left over from the district's last incarnation. In these trend-setting cultural cores, each shop sells objects and services that differ greatly in their detail, despite being essentially the same commodity: "creativity" as a lifestyle designation, delivered not via the specific use of the item but instead in the general application of "artisanal" character to a necessarily multivariate series of nonsensical products and services. It does not much matter if these districts are in Berlin, Shanghai, or Mexico City.

The same is true of a third urban dynamic: the rise of global sunbelts for manufacturing, logistics, and an array of bottom-rung "postindustrial" services such as call centers, new low-level digital work on click farms, or piecemeal programming outsourced to places like Hyderabad. Here, again, the parallels are remarkable. My first time living in China (in 2012) was spent in the southwest, largely in newly developed provincial capitals like Kunming and Nanning, which had exploded in size with the post-crisis stimulus, funding the construction of subways, highways, and high-speed rail, all of which was followed by a real estate boom sprawling past the outskirts of such cities in anticipation of new waves of industrial investment that to this day have failed to live up to expectations. In later years, I would move from the southwest to the southern coast, spending time in Guangzhou, Shenzhen, and Hong Kong (the three major economic centers of the Pearl River Delta) in the years after the wave of factory closures that followed the last global crisis. These cities were at the center of China's own early export-oriented sunbelt, constructed in the same years as the rise of its American counterpart in the Southern states and exhibiting a surprisingly similar geography of decentralized sprawl. The only difference is one of scale, with the American single-family unit or modest European high-rise replaced in this case by gargantuan residential towers.

Of all Chinese cities, Shenzhen stands out in this regard, since its development has been almost entirely concurrent with the opening of China to the global economy. Once nothing more than marshland surrounding a moderately sized market town, Shenzhen was designated China's first Special Economic Zone in 1980. It quickly became one of the industrial powerhouses of China's Pearl River Delta and then one of the fastest growing cities in the world. At first, industrial centers agglomerated around major access zones to Hong Kong, which was both an important source of capital and the primary gateway to global markets—migrants flooded into cheap, hastily built "urban villages" in places like Nanshan to work in factories and work-shops near the Shekou port. Soon rising real estate prices pushed industry outward, as places with closer proximity to the border became new service and financial centers, as well as settlement zones for wealthier foreigners. Once-rural townships and villages further north were able to attract increasing amounts of capital to build new factories and extensive infrastructure. As migrant workers flooded into such "villages," the original peasants' landholdings were effectively converted into shares within local capital projects. Meanwhile, massive skyscrapers were built along the border in Luohu, the Shenzhen stock exchange was opened in centrally located Futian, and hip bars, art galleries, and boutiques were opened in both the foreigner-friendly Overseas Chinese Town and within a redeveloped Shekou.[33]

Shenzhen and its urban rail system soon grew to encompass a number of other municipalities as more labor-intensive industry was pushed further and further out, driven by the early success of the liberalized township-and-village enterprises. But instead of a single, widening ring of industry followed by an expanding core of more affluent residential zones and service centers, the sprawl of the city was inherently uneven. New factories sprung up over paddy fields, and agriculture itself grew more intensive as it became more thoroughly integrated into the new industrial infrastructure, which provided unprecedented access to both domestic and international markets. Some areas were simply abandoned or sold off by peasant-tenants, left undeveloped, partially developed, or specifically designated as zones for greenery or marshland, often in conjunction with large residential projects wanting to sell their units with the guarantee of "natural" amenities to appeal to the upwardly mobile middle class.[34] After the financial crisis, even many of the newer industrial zones farther out from the urban core(s) were upgraded to capital-intensive, high-tech production, with the more labor-intensive work in the supply chain mostly located at the very end of the subway system in new administrative districts like Longhua, far to the north of the original border factories.

Traveling toward Longhua, one is not at first struck by the industrial character of the city, but instead by its greenery. Just beyond the bounds of the more affluent downtown cores, new residential complexes encircle shopping malls selling knockoff name brands to the lower-wage white-collar workers who can no longer afford to live in the central districts. Behind these are often large swaths of green space intercut every now and then by some anonymous industrial facility, which then gradually open again onto more sprawling industrial districts in the city's far north, which tend to be centered on railroad stations and major business parks housing the factories of large employers like Foxconn, where the iPhone is manufactured. The striking part of all this is how decentralized the city is, a phenomenon that locals and scholars soon began to refer to as "rural-urban integration" (*chengxiang yitihua*).[35] Traveling farther up towards neighboring Dongguan, small patches of agriculture alternate with undeveloped or abandoned marsh and jungle, into which are dropped seemingly random clusters of gleaming white apartment towers, shopping malls, dance clubs, factories, warehouses, brothels, and so on.

Outside of its several downtown cores and largest expanses of logistics and industrial activity, much of Shenzhen and the greater Pearl River Delta are simply hard to define as either urban or rural at all. Areas of marsh and jungle may have once been factories or rice paddies, now abandoned as the village was converted into a shareholder corporation managing the sale of industrial sites or residential units on a fraction of the old agricultural collective's land. In other areas, the greenery might be entirely transplanted for the express purpose of creating a desirable landscape for ex-urban residents. Rather than attempting to pin down what, exactly, is the proper outer border of such a city, it makes more sense simply to acknowledge that the old categories of urban, suburban, and rural may simply have less explanatory power for the contemporary capitalist city than they once had. Instead, we can define clear islands of affluence, encircled by a near hinterland composed of identifiable industrial-logistics expanses that gradually fade into a farther hinterland of agriculture, black markets, and (half-)abandoned fields, factories, and forests.

Sprawl

There was, then, a certain familiarity here. Despite the humid heat punctuated by the brief respite of typhoon rains, the feeling that I got traversing the Pearl River Delta was much the same as that felt crossing the Inland Empire on the way to Los Angeles, with its massive patchwork of alternating industrial and residential corridors finally giving way to a coastal hub for finance and the "creative" industries. The same capitalist imperatives that built Shenzhen have also driven every stage of urbanization in u.s. cities, after all, and it shouldn't be surprising that the urban structure of Los Angeles, Houston, Texas, or other Sunbelt metropolises roughly mirror those of their Chinese counterparts. Sprawl is the general tendency of capitalist urbanization. In a completely unconstrained environment, an ascendant city would ripple outward, the early industrial core redeveloped into a spectacular downtown, ringed by ever-receding, ever-shortening ridges of economic activity that, at the utmost frontier, finally fall away to nothing more than a gently quivering emptiness. But constraints exist, and they are fundamental to the forces driving urbanization in the first place. Sunbelts become rust belts, competition leads to the rise of new technologies that drive the growth of new industrial cores, and physical geography wields unquestionable influence on the location of industry and living space. Thus every city tends to sprawl and collapse in its own unique way.

Without any zoning laws to speak of, Houston, like Shenzhen, is capable of rapid change in response to market imperatives. It therefore approximates the general tendency in ways that other cities do not. Where countervailing factors are strongest, cities will either tend to hyper-aggregate or hollow out, even while they sprawl. Most coastal cities, alongside a few inland brain hubs, are able to cohere around relatively large downtown cores. San Francisco represents the apex of this trend, with the city's interior slums almost entirely eliminated—leaving the poor to a scattering of small, rent-controlled leftovers, the rest made to wander homeless through the corridors of multi-million-dollar condominiums. But this is only possible when economic, historical, physical, and serendipitous factors all combine to ensure the upward mobility of the city, and this lasts only as long as the industrial boom that undergirds it. The Rust Belt cities represent the opposite constraint, with Detroit a mirror-image inversion of San Francisco.

But most other cities have had less success than the coastal hubs and have also not suffered the same kind of multi-decade decline as the manufacturing powerhouses of the northeast. As automobile factories were closing in St Louis, Detroit, and Cleveland, new factories were being opened in cheaper "right to work" states like Alabama, South Carolina, Texas, and Georgia. Similar dynamics were evident in cities across the southwest and into the heartland. Industrial behemoths like Boeing began to decentralize their supply chains, closing down production units in Seattle only to reopen them in Southern California, Kansas, and South Carolina.[36] Population followed, as outflow from the northeast and Midwest was matched by moderate growth in the West and a population explosion across the "New South."[37] It is this period of re-industrialization (accompanied by a new oil boom) that has driven the growth of sprawling cities in the south and southwest. The geography of these cities can be best characterized not simply as a wealthy core interacting with a poor periphery, but instead as an archipelago of wealthy islands rising above an ocean of industrial sprawl.

Cheap land and cheap labor are the major imperatives shaping such industrial-urban development. Sprawl is not the direct goal of any of the firms or government bodies involved, nor is it a particularly efficient outcome produced by the supposed rationalizing power of the market. Sprawl is instead an ancillary effect of these driving imperatives, as the lateral extension of the city becomes much more lucrative than dense, vertical agglomerations. As new industrial facilities relocate to the region, new rings of infrastructure and working-class settlement ripple outward into the deserts, swamps, and humid forests of the Sunbelt. At its most extreme, the city is exploded into tens or even hundreds of small cores and strips centered on logistics hubs and corridors, housing developments, or geographical amenities. In some cases, this means extremely low density, as in Houston. In others, relatively high density is retained via large numbers of mid-sized, multi-unit complexes, but the overall effect is the same. This is the case in Los Angeles and the Inland Empire, an extremely suburban complex with weak urban cores compared to New York and Chicago, but one which nonetheless ranks as the city in the United States with the either highest or second-highest population density. This is because dense suburbs combine with a relatively under-aggregated urban core to drive the average upwards.[38] The conclusion to be drawn from this is blasphemy for most urban planners, but the fact remains: sprawl and density are simply not opposed.

Meanwhile, entirely new cores often accrete within the sprawl itself. Houston is a case in point. According to the regular Houston Area Survey conducted by Rice University, "Houston can actually be said to have five to eight downtowns, and eighteen centers of activity."[39] These centers include not only hubs within the urban core, or just logistics hubs in the surrounding industrial suburbs, but new mid-level centers of activity in places like The Woodlands and Sugar Land, once almost exclusively residential freeway suburbs spawned by postwar interstate construction. Many suburbs in American cities have attracted their own large, central, mixed-use development projects in order to advertise themselves as attractive, urbanized places—and even in cities as auto-centric as Houston and Los Angeles, such development has also been accompanied by (often successful) attempts to extend light rail systems and other public transit out to these new centers. Rather than countervailing factors, these many competition-driven contradictions are the driving force of sprawl, and the formation of new cores is simply yet another episode in the long history of capitalist urbanization.

Though newly constructed Chinese cities might today typify the ideal, it was in America, after all, that the truly capitalist city was inaugurated. The traditional, tight-knit urban cores of European cities were largely inherited from pre-capitalist patterns of medieval urbanization, which then experienced population growth correlated to the rise of mercantile regimes in the seventeenth and eighteenth centuries, all of which gave the early capitalist era in Europe a pre-made set of urban centers originally designed to serve very different economic imperatives. Though older American cities (beginning as second-order entrepôts for Europe) inherited some of this character, the vast majority of major u.s. metropolitan areas today were inaugurated and developed according to the imperatives of an explicitly capitalist market.

Chicago, St Louis, the Twin Cities (Minneapolis and St Paul, Minnesota) and other Middle-American and Midwestern centers, alongside a spare few centers on the West Coast such as San Francisco and early Los Angeles, formed their cores when technological limits to urban expansion were only just beginning to be lifted. These are therefore the earliest cities to develop via lateral sprawl, made possible by the invention of the streetcar. The early suburbs extended out in a "star-shape" from the city, following the rail lines, which would soon be superseded by highways capable of closing in the empty space between streetcar hubs. The result was that, by 1899 (prior to the widespread adoption of the automobile), "the population density of fifteen American cities was twenty-two persons per acre as compared to 158 for thirteen German cities."[40] Cheap, depopulated land allowed for an unprecedented extension of the city into the surrounding countryside.

By the latter half of the twentieth century, urbanization in America would become synonymous with sprawl. The outward pressure evident in the early streetcar suburbs was finally released with the widespread adoption of the automobile and federal support for the construction of a national road system, beginning with aid programs in the 1920s and '30s, before reaching its apex in the construction of the interstate system after the Second World War. This fundamentally changed the inter-urban geography of the country, essentially beginning the decentralized explosion of the city out along transit and logistics corridors: "Before 1920, there was no commerce along the highways between one city or town and the next." Instead, there was a "staccato alternation of open countryside and discrete town borders." But the explosion of road infrastructure to accommodate the automobile "changed the nature of highways," with new roadside businesses transforming them into "a location of commerce," which would, in turn, prepare the ground for new waves of urban expansion.[41]

In the postwar period these initial experiments in highway commerce were transformed into a sequence of massive real estate booms, in which new housing developments of the more homogenous type associated with "traditional" suburbia would dominate new construction, accompanied by the greenfielding of industrial, retail, and service hubs nearer these centers. As the homogenous and relatively affluent character of the postwar suburb has begun to collapse, however, the extension of logistics cores and other employment hubs has accelerated. Much of the industrialization in the cities of the New South is taking place in precisely these newly impoverished suburban zones, where both land and labor are cheap.

In fact, rather than the virtuous, pan-urban density preached by the urbanists, "revitalization" projects seem more consistently to produce small, extravagant green zones jutting out of the unstable hinterland like the walled-off military outposts of an occupying army. Again, this seems simply to be the character of capitalist urbanization, in which the never-ending expansion of value is matched by the expansion of the city and its industrial exoskeleton, the body of value fixed in place as dead labor, and the palaces of capital fortified against the monstrosities of the machine that they helm.

Disintegration

In the winter of 2012/13, I returned from southwest China to the United States just in time to face my riot charges and be sent to the work-release unit. This was also the period in which the nascent political scene in the city that had cohered around Occupy had entered its final stage of slow self-cannibalization. By the time I got out of jail, the rent had doubled and most of the reasonable people had moved away or simply disengaged, leaving nothing but the wingnuts and identitarians with their blood feuds waged by ever-smaller micro-factions. Little remained from those two or three wild years in which the potentials had at first seemed so limitless. In the end, I found myself back in those same inner-ring suburbs where I had stayed years before. My cellmates and I never made it to Vegas, of course—not even Reno. That's how things go. The small fragments of the communal that we're able to forge out of those extreme moments are then slowly, meticulously torn apart by the world. After jail, I eventually lost contact with them, saying that I was too busy when really my life was the same as theirs or yours, waking up too late, rushing to work to feed hours into some distant and hungry abstraction you can never quite see the shape of—and talking to how many people, really? Honestly, it was no different in Shenzhen, where

I'd later meet workers at the Foxconn plant or neighboring factory cities who lived essentially the same sort of lives, despite our different positions within the global labor hierarchy. Our existence is disintegrated into a million minuscule atoms of exchange, circulating between everything in a ruthless hail of prices, profits, and wages. All that's touched by this exchange begins to disintegrate into similar atoms cast across similar sprawls of infrastructure and faceless iterations of the same residential plot repeated indefinitely.

The thing about poverty in these suburbs is that it doesn't look like poverty, just as class doesn't look like class. There are no overspilling brick-built public housing towers, as in the inner-city ghettos of the past. But there is also nothing that looks much like the French *banlieue* or the British council estate. Instead we have "Main Street," the darling of every politician. These places still have the surface appearance of those uniquely American suburbs: each house tucked quietly onto its own plot of land, no front porch even to mediate between the public and private. The cul-de-sacs of SeaTac do not immediately appear to be sites of brewing class war. But Ferguson, Missouri, also looked nothing like inner city St Louis. It was instead a quaint heartland suburb, the epitome of social stability. In the ideological imaginary, such neighborhoods are still the hometown of the "silent majority," the core demographic supposedly lending support to the American project. But then, at the height of the economic "recovery," Main Street was burned to the ground.

Underneath that surface appearance of stability, such spaces today signify a proletariat unified only in its separation. The economic ascent that made the suburbs into sites of working-class upward mobility has disappeared, replaced now with a slow collapse. Today's normal thus inhabits the landscape of the past haphazardly. Poverty seems to disappear behind the picket fence. Class appears to dissolve in isolation. How many people, really, do we talk to in a given day? We talk to co-workers, customers, maybe crowds, depending on the job. Maybe it's one of those social positions—a teacher, a counselor, something in which you can at least lie to yourself for a while and say you're making some sort of impact, that you're at least able to *connect* with people. But those lies come harder when you've had some fragment of truly communal closeness, only to be thrown back into the world as it is—the material community of capital, where even our basic emotional connections are somehow mediated by that hostage situation we call the economy. It doesn't really matter if it's a riot, an occupation, or maybe just something preserved under the extreme circumstances of imprisonment and poverty. You can feel yourself losing it. After work, you go straight home to smoke some weed and watch a movie, or maybe you see a handful of friends who somehow still feel distant, cycling through the bar or the club desperately to try to force that feeling back, as if it were a kind of narrow chemical deficiency instead of an expansive social devastation. You get home somehow in the darkness, the dull orange glow of those factories and warehouses backlighting the horizon.

After the ash is pressure-washed off Main Street, and walls are erected around the black skeletons of burnt-out buildings, the illusion of stability sets back in, only now more fragile, guarded by more police. The return to normalcy is never really a return to anything—recognition of this fact is the only way you can escape the emotional ruin of these "recoveries." Each time less and less is actually recovered, and this leaves space for new, less controllable potentials. Behind the peeling paint of suburban stability, there are hidden sightlines aimed at the heart of the global economy. As Washington highway 509 runs south from the Duwamish to the working-class suburbs, it stretches up a heavily forested ridge between White Center and Burien. In recent years, this forest has become an intermittent homeless settlement, filled with people fleeing the renewed sweeps and encampment closures that have accompanied Seattle's "revitalization." Many of the southern suburbs, where homelessness was previously a rare phenomenon, have seen massive spikes of people squatting or living on the streets. The result is a suburban forest filled with squatters perched above a bustling industrial valley. Planes descend onto the airstrips, container trucks load and unload, trains roll sluggishly across traffic-choked thoroughfares—all of it simultaneously chaotic and choreographed, just reckless enough to pose the question: how long before the center gives again? Above, those tree-dwelling squatters peer down at the economy from which they've been excluded. Though it seems as though they're a mere handful of outcasts from the palace of the creative class, they themselves are really only the most visible forefront of that vast proletarian specter sealed out of sight for now in the warehouses and postwar homes of the new suburbia—until Main Street burns again.

four

Oaths of Water

St Louis is where storms collide. Without the moderating effect of a coastline or major mountain range, cold air sweeps unopposed down from the Arctic to meet a warm, humid front marching north from the Gulf of Mexico. The two finally lock in combat over the Mississippi flatlands, emptying their arsenals to barrage the area with blizzards, thunderstorms, and tornados. In recent years, growing climate chaos has only intensified this ambient war, each "extreme weather event" more volatile and less predictable. And as the air currents grapple over the middle-American sky, the storm-swollen Mississippi grinds forward below. Once-uncommon "freak floods" are now standard, the levees overcome every few years and large chunks of St Louis and its surrounding suburbs washed away by the intractable inertia of a river bound to outlive any city.

The result is another slow apocalypse. In January 2016, people from the surrounding suburbs poured into Red Cross shelters, unable to return to homes torn apart by the rising water. But even with such disasters gradually becoming the new, more violent equilibrium, federal aid is perpetually insufficient. The Red Cross itself was a minimal presence compared to the swarm of church groups sifting through the wreckage to offer disaster relief.[1] In a landscape of increasingly perpetual crisis, even the somewhat mundane organizing of church groups takes on an almost prophetic weight. Politics in these conditions can only appear apolitical, as all functional organizing is given political significance when confronted with devastation of such scale: Baptists and Mennonites organizing supply caravans through the wreckage of long-decayed postwar suburbs, the crosses emblazoned on their white vans floating above silt-clogged cul-de-sacs.

Such stories of environmental destruction are, however, only one dimension of a much-deeper global economic catastrophe that takes different forms in different regions. In many ways, St Louis is a city without a region, stuck between the Midwest, the South, and the Great Plains—and as such it seems to act as a sort of vaguely generalizable image of a mythic middle America slowly being lost. Economically, it's an intersection between Rust Belt and Corn Belt, only barely outside the new sunbelt yet falling short of its river-port counterparts. It was one of the many cities left behind by the wave of deindustrialization. After its postwar heyday, the entire metro area saw massive population loss, at first concentrated downtown but soon spreading out to neighboring suburbs as well. This process only deepened long-standing racial divides. Meanwhile, attempts to resuscitate the city by focusing on capital-intensive manufacturing and biotech have only ensured a further cloistering of wealth and a hardening of racial divides between neighborhoods.

Today postwar houses and small clusters of low-rise apartment complexes are sprinkled out across the humid floodplain. When the river overspills its levees, entire suburban cities can be washed away, as was the case in the small, predominantly white working-class suburb of West Alton in 2016. Wedged between the Missouri and Mississippi, just before their confluence north of St Louis proper, the entire city was evacuated, with a quarter to a third of the population expected never to return.[2] Even without the floods, economic pressures have created a different dynamic of flight and decay, as formerly white working-class suburbs such as Ferguson, Berkeley, and Florissant (all once demographically similar to West Alton) grow increasingly impoverished, the declining rents acting as a magnet for people attempting to move out of the inner-city slums in search of better schools and infrastructure. A new wave of white flight follows, in what is essentially an unprecedented expansion of the interior slum zone outward into a select few suburbs lying along major transit routes.

There are small islands of gentrification within the city proper, as well as the remains of more affluent suburbs, largely west of the city—the foremost of these being small municipalities like Town and Country, a largely white golf course suburb that boasts the highest median income of any city in Missouri. These richer locales are buffered by a spectrum of poorer ones, including largely white working-class suburbs and satellite cities such as St Charles and Alton, as well as cities like Florissant, once almost entirely white, now two-thirds white and one-third black. In some places, the spectrum between wealth and poverty is truncated, and the borders between areas of affluence and areas of absolute impoverishment are harsh. In others, the spectrum is wide, and a number of middle-income zones persist in the interstice between city and country. In St Louis, these divergent dynamics are colliding, and the city is being reshaped according to this economic battle, itself only an echo of that greater chaos foreboded by warring storms.

Ferguson, Missouri

I was in Ferguson years before the floods, weeks after the burning of the QuikTrip, and months before the burning of everything else.[3] People were still gathering on Florissant Avenue every night, undeterred by the alternating heat and rain or by the army of police that had been deployed to patrol the picket fences, geometric lawns, and big-box stores of the postwar suburb. The first round of riots was the only major uprising in an American suburb within living memory. And I was there in what was only a momentary lull, the eye of the storm. Walking around in the scorching heat through the low-hanging brick apartment complexes where Michael Brown was murdered, everyone I spoke with knew that nothing else would happen until winter. The verdict would be postponed until it was cold, the government hoping that the weather might deter another round of protests. But everyone was equally adamant that winter was not an issue. We can start our own fires, they said. And when it came, the second round of riots saw much of the suburb burn.

The perfect storm had been building for some time. Ferguson is at the bottom of the income spectrum and has acted as a sort of vanguard for the outward march of suburban poverty. Like many postwar suburbs, its heyday was in the 1950s and '60s, which saw successive doublings of the population until it reached a peak of nearly 30,000 in 1970. Deindustrialization beginning in the '70s was then matched with a continual drop in population to about 21,000 today, in line with St Louis's historic population loss. As the city grew smaller and poorer, its racial demographics also flipped. As late as the 1990 Census, Ferguson was still 73.8 percent white and 25.1 percent black (close to the proportions of neighboring Florissant today), but by 2010 this situation had entirely reversed (to 29.3 percent white and 67.4 percent black). Inflation-adjusted income dropped, and unemployment doubled from around 5 percent in 2000 to an average of 13 percent between 2010 and 2012.[4]

The political establishment reflected this history. At the beginning of the riots, the city government was helmed by a white mayor, a white police chief, and five white and one Hispanic city council people. Combined with this, the dwindling population, fleeing industry, and plummeting property values had created a budgetary crisis, forcing many of the area's small municipalities to rely less on their shrinking tax base and more on extra-tax fees and fines, enforced by the police and facilitated by the city's arcane court system. The result was that Ferguson and similar suburbs existed in what the *Huffington Post* called "a totalizing police regime beyond any of Kafka's ghastliest nightmares."[5] Out of a population of roughly 21,000, over 16,000 Ferguson residents had arrest warrants issued. And this number only counts individuals with warrants, not the total number of warrants. In 2013 this figure was a staggering 35,975, roughly 1.5 warrants per person in the city.[6] These warrants were part of a complex racket designed to impose unrelenting fines on the poor population in order to fund the city government, which itself had largely been redesigned to facilitate this predatory practice. In 2013 fines, court fees, and other such extortions accounted for some 20 percent of the city's budget. These fines were disproportionately applied to the city's black residents, with black drivers twice as likely to be stopped, searched, and arrested as their white counterparts.[7]

In one sense, this reflects the age-old pattern of racially uneven impoverishment common to American economic downturns. In the old industrial northeast, black workers were "last hired, first fired," and when the factories began to close, they were consistently given the worst deals in terms of severance pay, retirement, or new employment opportunities in the suburbs. The disproportionate racial character of policing in Ferguson and elsewhere in the u.s. is simply undeniable—facts attested to with a bloody consistency by incarceration rates and the likelihood of police murder. But overemphasizing these features can also obscure the broader trend, which is distributed along class lines even while this distribution is disproportionately distorted according to race. This is most obvious in zones of white rural poverty, as mentioned in earlier chapters. But it is also apparent in the white–black divide of the St Louis area, where the white working class is faring only a little better than its black counterpart. In fact, Ferguson was only ranked third in the area for its predatory financial system, trailing behind the majority-white working-class suburbs of St Ann (39.6 percent) and St John (29.4 percent) in its dependence on extortion.[8]

These funding systems are not unique to St Louis, but instead became a national trend as more and more municipalities found themselves in dire conditions after the last crisis. The suburban-ization of poverty and skyrocketing incarceration rates have thus been paired with growth in these massive, extra-tax extortions applied to the poor—and particularly the suburban and rural poor, who are more likely to live in small, cash-strapped muni-cipalities (or counties) with a dwindling tax base and less access to federal aid. In most places, this takes the form of an expanding net of legal search, supervision, and harassment that essentially extends the walls of the prison out into the new suburban ghetto. Increasingly expensive incarceration is gradually replaced by a predatory probation system composed of extra-carceral monitor-ing, fines, and seizure of property, all amplified by the fusion of public budgets and for-profit probation companies.[9]

Many of these are relatively recent trends, with Ferguson's dependence on probation funding skyrocketing after 2010.[10] But rather than an unfortunate exception, Ferguson is a window into the future. As low growth, deepening crisis, and general austerity continue, more of the new ghettoes will find themselves strug-gling for shares of a shrinking tax base. These cities will be forced to find new sources of funding, and the easiest way to do this is for better-off residents to utilize existing legal resources in order to prey on the poor. As the economic situation becomes increas-ingly dire, similar patterns emerge at greater scales: the county, the state, and the federal government will all turn to such predatory practices, facilitated by growing armies of police and preexisting legal mechanisms for debt collection, surveillance, and incarceration.

These patterns are piloted in the poorest areas, applied first to the most disadvantaged social groups. In Anaheim, California, the poorer, predominantly Latino neighborhoods in the city have

seen a series of gang injunctions, allowing plainclothes police
to arrest and open fire on residents for things as simple as their
clothing color or gathering in a crowd. In 2012 a sequence of
police shootings in the city led to nights of rioting just outside
Disneyland.[11] In the poorer parts of New York, stop and frisk
policies and the enforcement of laws against minor offences
(such as selling loose cigarettes) have allowed for similar practices, resulting in local riots around the killing of Kimani Gray
in Flatbush in 2013 and national riots around the killing of Eric
Garner in 2014.[12] Similar practices have long been applied to the
rural poor, including the black residents of regions such as the
Mississippi River Delta, Native residents of reservations such as
Pine Ridge, Latino farmworkers across the country, and the white
poor in places like the coal-mining towns of Appalachia. The difference today is simply that these pilot programs are generalizing
at the same time that the demographic inversion pushes the poor
into the underfunded near-hinterland of sprawling suburbia.

Suburban Warfare

There were maybe ten police for every person on the street. They
formed lines to keep people walking an interminable circle on the
sidewalk. They stood in clusters in the background, commanders
from the state patrol talking with equivalent authorities drawn
from the local departments. Even more were deployed out of
sight: mostly bored soldiers from the National Guard scrolling
through Facebook next to armored vehicles parked in front of
Target or Ross Dress for Less. They flew above us in drones. They
walked among us in plain clothes. Some drove by in unmarked
suvs, "black leadership" from local churches and ngos sitting next
to them, pointing out the "troublemakers." Amid all of this, the
most oppressive force remained the scorching Missouri sun, its
light shattering down onto the pavement like hot metal. Those
not deterred by the heat shuffled under it in shifts, retreating

periodically to the nearby McDonald's for shade and water. People drove by with their phones held out the open windows of air-conditioned cars. A teenager in town for a national meeting of the Model UN asked me to take a picture of him in front of the fenced-off ruins of the QuikTrip for his Snapchat story.

I'd gone to Ferguson with a small group of friends who worked on shared political projects, all of whom had met through Occupy. Just a few weeks after the initial uprising and a couple days before Mike Brown's funeral, the small city was swarmed with people. Most of these were journalists or activists driven in by NGOs, often funded by hefty grants from church groups and liberal philanthropists. There was also the Revolutionary Communist Party (RCP), with its army of bullhorns and crazy-eyed followers.[13] While most of these groups were there to catch some screen time on CNN or harvest fresh meat for the Ford Foundation and the cult of Avakian, they hardly fit the media's favored image of the "outside agitator." We, on the other hand, were fashionably black-clad white people from the West Coast. With good cardio and edgy politics, we were outside agitators par excellence.

But we hadn't flown all that way to waste our time spitting into bullhorns and walking in circles. There was no need to explain how the police were bad and how life was fucked—these were already salient facts. The unrest was in a lull until the verdict, and no amount of forcing would hasten the next round. Many who lived in the town were busy breaking leases and packing their belongings, fully aware that in a few months the entire city would burn. So we weren't really there to agitate, but simply to observe how politics and repression might play out in our era's first major revolt in the American hinterland. This was something utterly unique, a picture of our future as poor people consigned to urban fringes and inner-ring suburbs. The driving questions were, how does a riot grow in this decentralized space, and what limits its growth? Can a new communist politics emerge from capitalist sprawl?

As the miserable Missouri sun set, a new energy seemed to mobilize alongside the encroaching darkness. The crowd would grow as the air cooled, adrenaline buzzing as contact was amplified between so many strangers aligned against the police. It became clear that darkness—one of the key components of riots everywhere—takes on an added significance here. Driving through Ferguson, Florissant, Berkeley, and other St Louis suburbs at night, the first thing one is struck by is the simple density of the night, full of humid air and hissing insects. Most of the highways are not lined with streetlights, and many residential streets are lit more by the intermittent glow of porch lights fading quickly against a border of hot, weed-choked blackness.

Throughout history, streetlights have been used as tools in riot prevention, and their earliest implementation in the coal gas lamps of Great Britain was closely allied with the simultaneous deployment of London's early police force. In 1785 the *London Chronicle* proclaimed that "Light and watch are the greatest enemies to villains," and by 1823 the newly professionalized night watchmen would be accompanied by "nearly forty thousand lamps" that "lit more than two hundred miles of London's streets."[14] When Baron Haussmann redesigned Paris after the uprisings of 1848, wide, well-lit boulevards were a centerpiece of his strategy for riot control.[15] In the u.s. the redeveloped inner city has followed an almost identical pattern. Dense, narrow-all eyed warehouse districts and project housing were demolished to make way for wide, brightly lit boulevards sprinkled with surveillance cameras. After the anti-World Trade Organization riots in Seattle, much of the city's downtown was renovated by a new round of real estate development led by the billionaire Paul Allen. Trash cans and newspaper boxes were chained to the sidewalk, thoroughfares were widened, and most of the dark, circuitous industrial territory on the central city's north edge was bulldozed, replaced with condo towers and Amazon's gleaming bio-dome headquarters. Similarly, in New York the last remnants of the old, dangerous city were reformatted into public spaces comfortable enough for the enjoyment of the elite, such as the conversion of an old New York Central Railroad spur into Manhattan's elevated High Line Park.

But the suburbs were never designed for riot prevention. They are under-lit, under-surveilled, and under-policed. When the riots broke out in Ferguson, they were confronted with a police department of only 53 officers, fifty of whom were white and none of whom had any training in riot suppression, counterterrorism, or the operation of the military equipment that had been bequeathed to them.[16] Compare this to New York, where the riots in Flatbush in 2013 and over the killing of Eric Garner in 2014 were met with the New York Police Department (NYPD), the world's seventh-largest standing army. These riots were quickly and deftly suppressed by well-trained tactical squads operating on an urban battlefield that had literally been built for them. This resilience operates on more levels than just the efficient monopolization of force, however. When confronted with claims of racial bias, the NYPD could easily turn to its own internal diversity in defense. When two officers were shot in Brooklyn in 2014 by Ismaaiyl Brinsley (ostensibly in revenge for the killings of Eric Garner and Michael Brown), the department quickly pointed out that the officers (Rafael Ramos and Wenjian Liu) were not white, using the incident to push for police to be protected under a hate crime law.[17] When another NYPD officer, Peter Liang, shot and killed Akai Gurley, an unarmed black man, many local Asian Americans even mobilized in a series of protests defending Liang, rather than Gurley.[18]

These events hint at the fact that the policing apparatus in many central cities extends far beyond the borders of the police department itself. A key element of riot suppression in these places has been the mobilization of a vast array of non-profits, church groups, activist organizations, and progressive wings of city government to encourage an "end to the violence." After the killing of Kimani Gray in Flatbush, the first few nights of rioting were met largely by the presence of the NYPD, which used traditional riot suppression techniques to break up the main body of protestors and make sweeping arrests. But softer forms of suppression soon followed, with Councilman Jumaane Williams and non-profits such as Fathers Alive in the Hood (FAITH) arriving to blame people from "outside the community" for the violence, driving a wedge between the black youth who had been leading the riots night to night and the array of radicals who had come out to support them.[19]

In Baltimore a similar sequence unfolded in 2015. After widespread repression on the part of police, the riots were capped by a series of arsons, including a church and a non-profit-funded senior center. The NGO response makes their policing function clear:

> In a curious twist of cause and effect, the riots provided a means of blaming this already-existing austerity *on the rioters themselves*. During the fires, community leaders went on-air to say that they had no idea why the youths would burn the very infrastructure on which their futures depended. Pastor Donte Hickman Sr. (pastor of the church that burned) argued on CNN that the rioters were "insensitive to what the church and the community was doing here," and that the focus needs to be "on how we rebuild." Other news programs underlined how the fires and looting would destroy services and jobs, taking money away from schools and recreation centers, and keeping the poor in the same state of austerity they brought upon themselves in the first place.[20]

These talking points are largely consistent with those used by progressives in New York and elsewhere, who hope, through peaceful protest, to attract the attention of elite saviors capable of restoring their "communities" from the outside: "With his church still in flames, Hickman pled for 'private investors to come in to East Baltimore and change it for the better.'"[21] Others uphold a more self-sufficient philosophy:

> within the riots themselves the most reactionary protestors were the senior Bloods, Crips, and Nation of Islam members who guarded storefronts, called for peace and order and even stood between protestors and police. . . "We don't really need [the police]," said one Bloods member, "We can do this ourselves. We can police them ourselves."[22]

In both New York and Baltimore, the hard repression of the police department is clearly accompanied by the soft suppression dealt by an equally vast and equally vicious apparatus of non-profits, progressives, churches, and reactionary religious, nationalist, or criminal groups, all of whom have strong vested interests in the currently existing distribution of power.

They represent one pole of the changing racial structure of the u.s., and are often operating on behalf of recently elevated non-white fractions of the local upper class. These fractions are positioned such that they perceive themselves to be threatened both by the entrenched old-money white bourgeoisie and simultaneously by the building unrest in the lowest rungs of their own racial "communities." Their assumed connection to these "communities" provides a certain legitimacy and plays an important ideological role, even while they often seek meticulously and thoroughly to sever any substantial connection with the lower class. Despite otherwise substantial differences, then, each of these sects mobilizes in its own way to suppress any violent break with normalcy, even while speaking of police reform and the redistribution of wealth, often conceived as simply the elevation of a more equitable share of non-whites into the ruling class. The key to understanding these dynamics is not attempting to sort such groups by their professed beliefs—which vary widely—but instead to analyze their actions when confronted with such uprisings. In this respect, they all behave in an almost identical fashion, as ancillaries of the police.

In Ferguson, however, a grassroots "black leadership" was almost entirely absent. Without local church groups, non-profits, or black cops and city council members, the government had to ship in a liberal leadership wholesale from neighboring St Louis, throwing in Al Sharpton for good measure. The governor appointed black highway patrol captain Ronald Johnson temporary commander of the local police department, and officers were ordered to march alongside the black liberals bused in by civil rights NGOs. Johnson himself was soon pictured hugging protestors in staged photo-ops, attempting to send a message of peace and reconciliation. But the effect of this soft counterinsurgency was diminished because it had no truly local roots. Despite the attempt of elderly civil rights leaders and their young crop of Americorp-bred, Ivy-League-educated, middle-class-POC apprentices to act as the universal leadership of the "black community," the reality is that no such community exists. Despite shared race, there are few other unifying factors tying this outside leadership to the rioters themselves. When Jesse Jackson's motorcade showed up in front of the McDonald's on Florissant, he was quickly confronted by a crowd of protestors yelling for him to "go home." The soft counterinsurgency seemed just as inept as the Ferguson police, and only a few days after the staged hugs, the governor was declaring a state of emergency. Deployment of the National Guard followed, dropping any pretense of gentle recuperation.

The other features that extended the riots in Ferguson were largely artifacts of the area's own affluent past: the lack of surveillance, its decentralization, the ease with which rioters could move between street, forest, and fenced-in yard. Quite unlike the narrow street-and-alley geography of the urban riot, this suburban unrest had an enormous amount of space within which to operate—the main constraint was not the police or the physical obstruction of traffic and buildings, but instead the long, flat distance between decentralized targets. The police tried to use this space to their advantage, forcing the protestors to march in an unending circle up and down the suburban strip, rather than kettling them or otherwise hindering their motion. But it was difficult truly to control such a large territory, and when the National Guard arrived, they were largely seen protecting big-box stores or other presumed targets, rather than attempting to patrol the entire area.

It was also impossible to constrict the flow of people to the protests via public transit shutdowns—another common feature of urban riot control. Relatively few people were dependent on public transit in Ferguson, and the city has no central transit center or rail link that could be shut down. Cars quickly became an integral part of the protest, something almost completely unseen in urban unrest but remarkably natural in a town where 79.8 percent of workers commute alone in a personal vehicle, according to census data. Vehicles were used not only as a means of quick transportation, but as a method to intensify the energy at different nodes of the riot. People gathered on top of cars, rode in slow circles around the strip and blasted Lil Boosie's "Fuck the Police" at the police.

On top of this was the use of Molotov cocktails and widespread reports of people shooting at the police—all greatly assisted by the abundance of dark, greenery-covered spaces for preparation and escape. When the arsons began in the second wave of rioting (in November), it was fairly straightforward for people to target particular buildings and then flee to nearby tree cover (either disappearing or, according to some reports, firing warning shots at the firefighters who came to put the fire out). The abundance of suburban side streets enabled a quick getaway, with or without a vehicle. All of these features allowed the Ferguson riots to be the longest wave of unrest seen since last century's ghetto riots.

Dead Labor

St Louis and its surrounding cities are built on a series of bluffs and terraces rising over the lowest segments of the Mississippi floodplain, all layered on a bedrock of limestone and dolomite laid down during the aptly named Mississippian age, when waters covered much of the Northern Hemisphere. Rock beds from such aquatic epochs tend to be dominated by carbonate sedimentary deposits left behind by long-dead oceans—a combination of evaporated salts and the multitude of corpses left by extinct marine organisms. Such deposits are a spare record of an alien earth, where land gave way to water and worlds drowned in the dark, historyless expanse of deep time. And today, in a strange, mindless echo, such deposits tend to be defined by the flow of water. Limestone and dolomite are particularly soluble rocks, easily dissolved by exposure to the mild acidity of groundwater. Though their surfaces often lack large bodies of sitting ponds and lakes, this is because rainfall and floodwaters quickly seep through joints in the limestone to flow through underground rivers and fill hidden reservoirs. Areas dominated by such deposits are often defined by water-cut karst topographies— pillars, caves, gorges—and expansive underground aquifers. In the u.s., roughly 40 percent of drinking groundwater comes from karst aquifers despite karst only composing 20 percent of its land mass. Globally, more than a quarter of the world's population either lives on or draws water from karst aquifers.[23]

The remains of dead oceans therefore gestate new ones, growing slowly in the darkness through the trickle of rainwater into lightless chambers beneath the earth. Dead things have a way of coming back. Before Ferguson, racial unrest was supposed to have been conclusively beheaded by the joint success of Civil-Rights-era institutional reforms and the subsequent expansion of the policing and prison apparatus. We were told that this victory had created a "post-racial" America, in which a black president could preside over the world's largest prison population, and ghetto riots were a thing of the past—Los Angeles '92 being nothing but a late-stage echo of this decisive defeat. But then after Ferguson there was Baltimore; there was Minneapolis; there was New York again; and there was Baton Rouge, Louisiana; Milwaukee, Wisconsin; and Charlotte, North Carolina. And these were only the most notable in a wave of discontent flooding from the Rust Belt out to every coast. Ferguson could not be written off as Los Angeles was in '92 as a late outlier. Instead it marks a sort of tectonic shift recognized across the political spectrum—the moment when something fissured and the first rushes of cold, dark water started pouring forth from long-buried aquifers.

While Occupy Wall Street several years prior had hinted at the possibility, the events in Ferguson guaranteed that the u.s. would not be immune to the return of the historical party. The form of this return (evidenced by the increasing violence and depth of global unrest) is fundamentally shaped by the character of production, since the character of production sculpts the character of class, and class conflict is, at bottom, the driving force of such unrest. In the present, the riot is both the natural evolution of otherwise suffocated struggles and a constituent limit in expanding or advancing such struggles beyond narrow territories and brief windows of time. Ferguson, then, is the unambiguous entry of the United States into a global era of riots. And this global era of riots is itself an outcome of the current extent and composition of the material community of capital, an always collapsing, always adapting edifice built from strata of dead labor, fissured now and again by the tectonic force of crisis and class conflict.

People in Ferguson therefore had to grapple with practical questions of cohesion and organization in a thoroughly atomized environment, just as those in Occupy did—a less developed though significant precursor. Alongside deindustrialization, the global workforce has, in general, been pushed away from direct access to the factories, farms, and machinery that build our world. As automation has grown more complex and computerized, production itself is split into minute segments coordinated by inscrutable algorithms, all overseen by a highly skilled workforce of specialized laborers and engineers, themselves constantly being made redundant by new waves of computerization. Even where manual laborers still toil in factories and workshops, they do so in shrinking numbers and as only one link in a globe-spanning supply chain, with little knowledge of the stages that precede or follow their particular factory. More of the workforce is to be found today in service and logistics, outside the "immediate process of production," where capital meets labor to produce new value. And even these new occupations are increasingly part-time, temporary, or simply insufficient. The proletariat thus returns to something more akin to its original condition, defined more by its dispossession than its privileged access to the gears of the world as an industrial workforce. Both Ferguson and Occupy, then, were early experiments in how proletarian factions might operate within the widening fields of competitive control being opened by the Long Crisis.

And this is not a field in which industry has somehow disappeared. As the previous chapters have shown, the opposite is true: today industry is more expansive than ever, reshaping the globe in an unprecedented wave of urbanization that has all but eliminated the "countryside" or "wilderness" as a space marginally outside the capitalist mode of production. The primary form that this takes is the expansion of a network of logistics infrastructure across the hinterland—at its most dense in the near hinterland on the outskirts of major metropolitan zones, growing to thin strands or spare nodes the farther one travels out into the farms and opiate-scarred wastelands of the far hinterland. The proletariat, though largely dispossessed of privileged access to the inner chambers of the economy's beating heart, is nonetheless distributed across all of its major veins and arteries. Due to its relative industrial density, the near hinterland will likely be the central theater in the coming class war, the most concise summation of which is simply the fact that large populations of people who have been made surplus to the economy live and work along its integral corridors. Dead labor, too, has a way of coming back.

The Squares

The thing that people get most consistently wrong about Seattle is the rain. Watch movies or TV shows set in the area, and the rain is always shown barreling down in thick torrents, dialogue sinking into its ambient roar as the water soaks through people's clothes until all the characters are just hauling layers of dark but mildly fashionable North Face fleeces and charcoal-colored hoodies on their shoulders, physically yoked to their directors' heavy-handed metaphors. The truth, though, is that the rain hardly even falls. It just hangs in a slow drizzle, heavier in some areas, lighter in others, disappearing and reappearing at a moment's notice as the whim of the many microclimates shifts unpredictably. In most seasons, it's simply ambient—a thin atmosphere of mist plummeting in slow motion. It doesn't soak you in one large, catastrophic wave, like the torrential downpours of our sister rainforests in the tropics. Instead, it joins with the darkness of the northern winter to grind you down with a miserable, slow indifference. Your clothes don't soak through in a single storm, but after a month or two, nothing seems capable of fully drying, and you've forgotten when it got wet in the first place. Then the mold comes, and that deep, bone-cold you get from a winter that hangs just above the edge of freezing. You remember that the water in a frozen lake is coldest not near the dried-out ice on the surface but instead at the lightless bottom, where the liquid settles as its chemical pandemonium grows lethargic, constrained by the vacuum of dead energy and the pressure of the water overhead, capable of pushing benthic currents well below the atmospheric freezing point.

The last time I needed an umbrella was in the fall and winter of 2011 when Occupy Seattle was still Occupying something. At first the camp was in Westlake Park, in the middle of a "public square" that was neither public nor square, but instead a sort of angular polygon jammed in the middle of a high-end shopping center. The occupation grew in fits and spurts, and was spectacularly evicted on two different occasions for the same droll reasons of "public safety" offered elsewhere, largely at the behest of groups like the downtown business council, who feared that a bunch of indebted twenty-somethings and the myriad homeless people who gravitated to the camp might threaten the sanctity of their shopping district. The umbrellas were as much for the pepper spray as for the rain, and between the evictions, the police started confiscating them en masse. Alongside the revival of obscure anti-mask laws to prosecute protestors in places like New York, the Seattle umbrella ban was justified in terms of vague wording about the erection of "structures" within the park. The umbrellas were technically "structures," claimed the police, and thereby subject to confiscation. This was part of a good cop, bad cop game played by the city government, in which the mayor's office and a whole array of liberal NGOs would flock to the camp in the morning, handing out leaflets and offering to "host" the camp at City Hall, where it could "speak truth to power" directly and "begin the dialogue." Then, at night, the police would move in, also under orders from the mayor.

This is Seattle politics in a nutshell, and it is remarkably effective. Most unrest in the city is easily contained through continual police presence paired with abysmally long periods of "process" and "dialogue" that function like a war of attrition, similar to the way the judiciary process operates for the poor—a nominally fair and open system that is only really functional for those with the right connections and an excess of time. The rest plea out. The war never looks like a war, and there is no point at which any given battle is decisively lost. In a strange inversion of roles, the political apparatus itself operates with the fluidity of a guerrilla force, receding before the oncoming marches and ceding territory to be occupied. Meanwhile, it encircles and lures its opponent into an overextended foray across inhospitable terrain, fragmenting the opposing force and absorbing the edges that split off. It sequesters the danger in Potemkin villages and empty cathedrals of power: city halls, parliaments, parks, and shopping centers—all the while transforming what was an occupation into a siege, and when the time is right, moving in with a ruthless efficiency. Afterward there was not even a war. There was a dialogue. We all agreed on the fundamentals. Occupy Wall Street raised important questions. The websites of the mayor's office and city council members now have a section for wealth inequality on their drop-down menus.[24]

After the first two evictions downtown, it was decided that the camp should relocate to the campus of a local community college in the nearby Capitol Hill neighborhood, an old counter-cultural holdout rapidly being converted into a hip location for "creatives." This decision was nominally made by the "General Assembly," debated late into the rain-spattered night, pros and cons intercut with the incoherent babbling of screaming wingnuts dutifully repeated by the audience acting as "people's mic." Recalling it today, these audience-echoed debates seem insane, the kind of feeling I imagine a former cult-member gets recalling his life on the compound. This isn't true of everything in Occupy—most memories of it shrouded in the perfume of a half-remembered, briefly exciting if ultimately disappointing party—but it is particularly salient when remembering the General Assemblies and everything else associated with the passion play of "direct democracy," performed more for the public eye than for any functional value.

The truth is that decisions in Occupy were never made democratically, though they were direct. The General Assembly was not a decision-making body, even though its social essence lay in its own claim to be just this. Instead it was the pulpit in a church founded by dispossessed millennials, attracting its fair share of wingnuts and older converts. It was a space where one could publicly say all the things that had been welling up over the years but somehow remained unspoken amid the day-to-day drudgery of two foreign wars and a global economic collapse. Because of this, it remained fairly inchoate: a fountain of gut-feeling and undeveloped ideas, hemmed by the incessant, miserable pattering of the drum circle. The repetition of the people's mic made the speaker feel listened-to and instilled a basic element of emotional parity between pulpit and audience. For once it seemed that the recognition of our world for what it is was not a lonesome fact grasped in darkness but instead one of the spare few things that we truly shared with others: a communal hatred toward that monstrous material community of capital within which we'd all been born and bred.

The myth of direct democracy was promoted widely by its true believers, whose fanaticism united them across otherwise unbridgeable divides between "anarchist" and "liberal." While Chris Hedges could debate David Graeber on the finer points of property destruction, both shared a devotion to the movement's populist deity: the 99 percent. This deity conveniently spoke through the congregation itself ("We are the 99%"), reviving a long tradition of immanent theology that has often interwoven itself with the emergence of nascent communist politics. But beneath the populist gospel and the nightly sermons of the dispossessed, material forces were grinding away, determining the array of probabilities that would define the direction of the Occupation. In order to understand the emergence of some sort of communist politics between the opacity of the riot and the hyper-transparent jubilation of Occupy, it's necessary to examine the concrete ways in which the movement advanced and receded.

In reality, decisions were made by relatively small groups of people operating outside the public eye, united by affinities that had either been present before the Occupation or had been built up haphazardly within it. These groups sorted and re-sorted several times over the course of the movement, but this sorting was mostly a process of ejecting those who disagreed with the fundamental unifying principle of these groups, which was simply the advance and defense of the Occupation. Those who capitulated to the city's many offers of truce were gradually banished from these small decision-making bodies, and thereby failed to serve the function of a co-opted leadership despite their continued presence at the camps. In some instances, the small grouplets pushing the Occupation forward were largely tactical in nature. In many cities these fractions were composed of juggalos and street kids, whose long-standing opposition to the police helped to advance various Occupations beyond the stage of marching on sidewalks and claiming that the police pepper-spraying us were also "part of the 99%." In other instances, these grouplets were more strategic, leading the Occupation through the planning of things like camp relocation, bank occupations, or the port shutdowns. It was here that political affinities became marginally important, as many of these strategic advances were led by groups that had at their core people who had come together in previous years around protests against police murders—particularly those of John T. Williams in Seattle and Oscar Grant in Oakland. The internal stability of the camp was sustained, meanwhile, by equally small groups of people committed to finding food, running communal kitchens, doing basic cleaning, and offering whatever services they could. In these cases, people were often brought together by the camp itself, with some infrastructural support offered by those who had experience in charities and social work.[25]

This phenomenon was not unique to the Occupy movement in the U.S., but seems to have been a sort of general organizational principle spanning the Arab Spring and European Movement of the Squares, as well as later events in Turkey, Ukraine, Brazil, and Hong Kong. It is in the pragmatic function of such small groupings that we begin to observe a shift from historical to formal party. At times, this overlaps with the formation of the anti-party of the far right, as in Ukraine. But more often this shift seems to stall in an apparently apolitical terrain, where the tactical necessities of the struggle itself define the character of one's partisanship. In such situations, it's impossible to characterize participants by any political ideology or to correlate activity to identity.

A case in point is the role played by football gangs in the Squares Movement and North African insurrections. The football Ultras, who had a long history of street fighting experience and sometimes incorporated a (not always left-wing) vaguely political edge into their work, doubling as antifa groups and attracting exiled communist guerrillas or acting as youth wings for various nationalist projects,

> are a small, hard-core, organized, violent minority within a much larger and more diverse movement—an urban vanguard, as it were. Their tight cohesion, self-synchronizing swarming behavior, willingness to engage in violence, and battle-hardened tactical competence in the scrappy business of street fighting combine to give this radical subset of fans a great deal of latent military strength.[26]

Because of this, the Ultras were able to lead tactical advances that ultimately pushed the constellation of riots and protests into outright insurrection. Where Ultra clubs were most established and most experienced, the state had a much harder time suppressing nascent uprisings.

I therefore use "ultras" in the lower case to refer to all of those small grouplets enmeshed in larger struggles who wield some sort of "latent military strength," unified by something other than basic political agreement and who operate to advance and defend the potentials opened by recent unrest. In this sense, the ultras are active, non-state forces that operate within the more volatile spaces of competitive control—but their true distinguishing feature is a self-reflexive connection to particular local sequences of struggle, in which their actions are specifically partisan actions aimed at widening the potentials of the struggle and pushing it forward on behalf of and alongside the larger crowd. This mass element distinguishes them from the simple minority intervention of warlords, gangsters, or religious fundamentalists, though it is perfectly natural for such grouplets to devolve into similar formations when the greater struggle atrophies. Though generally aligned with the "Party of Anarchy" at the height of the unrest, ultras are defined by an apolitical pragmatism, seeking the maximal program of action capable of spreading the unrest across greater territories and driving it deeper into the structure of society. As formal parties gestate within the historical party, it is just as possible for ultras to turn to the right, joining the anti-party, as it is for them to retain fidelity to the Party of Anarchy. It is this polar volatility that makes such apolitical groupings central to the political outcomes of greater struggles.

The Streets

I never understood the need for umbrellas until I went to Hong Kong. There, the rain is torrential. Humid tropical sunlight is cut open by heavy clouds, the edge of the typhoon visible from the distance like a great fissure across the city—severing the sun-glittering skyscrapers of the main island from the clusters of New Town public housing built in the jungle near the border. Li Ka-Shing's port and all the glass buildings sitting on the land he purchased in the wake of the '67 riots are divided from the rooftop shanties and torturously subdivided closets housing the city's poor. The rain divides the steak houses from the noodle carts, Mandarin from Cantonese, and the streets from the alleys. It's little surprise, then, that the umbrella would soon become the symbol of a crowd capable of traversing that divide.

Oddly enough, there are no proper football hooligans in the former British colony. When the riots came in late 2014—building after years of soft populist protest led by old "pan-democrats"—they were thus led not by football Ultras but instead by ultras in the lower case. This took many forms, most of which were apolitical (though they were ultimately utilized as a stepping-stone for the far right).[27] Construction workers, skilled in the careful weaving required to build the city's signature bamboo scaffolding used on construction sites, came together to craft intricate meshwork barricades out of the same material, essentially converting a tool of the elite—for whom real estate is a key investment in one of the most expensive cities in the world—into a weapon against the police attempting to protect the very property values that the construction workers had helped to create. In other cases, the forms of affinity were smaller and simpler. Groups of like-minded friends smashed the windows of parliament. Others built shields emblazoned with images of Guan Yu, patron deity of police and gangsters, again inverting the tools of power against its practitioners. But throughout the Umbrella Movement, the ultras had found themselves in conflict with a large mass of traditional activists advocating peaceful protest, and such tactical advances only occurred at the margins, surrounded by controversy. By 2016, however, these forms of small-scale coordination would become almost second nature, as people rapidly mobilized against a crackdown on street hawkers in Mong Kok. Protestors brought shields and goggles, hurled projectiles at police, set fire to trash cans, and built barricades across major thoroughfares.

Each of these examples hints at one of the essential characteristics of the ultra that defines them in opposition to the activist: they raise the question of concrete power, instead of politics as proper language, proper analysis, or simply the act of being proper and respectable in the face of the police. We therefore come full circle, returning to the oath as the present form of partisanship, its pragmatic focus on the functional abilities of an engaged minority capable of at least temporarily cutting across an otherwise-unbridgeable atomization. For these partisans, there is often no self-conceived "politics," or at least no political strategy as such, only power and the tactics that build it. Counterinsurgency theorists like Kilcullen see this in purely military terms, and the average leftist sees in it only the specter of fascism. There is truth to both of these dimensions, of course. Since such grouplets can become "a politically biddable, readily mobilized, self-organized, street-savvy, battle-hardened *corps d'élite* in urban conflict," as Kilcullen says of the football Ultras, it is certainly not coincidental that they have played equal roles in both emancipatory insurrections (as in Egypt) and brutal sequences of violence (as in the Balkan Wars), as well as more politically ambiguous events that nonetheless have slanted toward the far right (as in Ukraine).[28]

But this doesn't make the phenomenon purely military or inherently fascist. In fact, this illusion is often the concrete cause of such rightward turns. In Hong Kong, leftists decried the actions of youth who smashed the windows of parliament, imagining that such violence was inherently opposed to the aims of the movement. Many of the youth who supported the action, therefore, began a slow turn towards the right, since right-wing localists were some of the only people who supported and defended these more violent advances.[29] The left's refusal to engage with these partisans is often the guarantee that turns the apolitical to the far right, since all varieties of nationalist, fascist, or simply authority-loving strongmen will have no qualms about organizing amid groups that have expressed minimal amounts of strength and discipline. The leftist, however, tends to quiver in the face of the juggalo screaming "faggot" at the cops or the black youth who brings a pistol to the memorial march.

The specter of fascism arises here because both the pre-political ultras and the resurgent right share the pragmatic focus on power and understand themselves as defined primarily by activity, rather than analysis. They both perceive their field of operation as one of competitive control, where political support follows strength, not vice versa. Neither have programs, but both adhere to the oath as an organizing principle. Leftists (and most specifically those whom the far right in Hong Kong quite appropriately took to calling "leftist pricks") demand a program as a necessary preface to "political" action, or simply presume that one will emerge naturally out of the activity of particular demographics. The absence of such a program is seen as an inherently fascistic elevation of might in the place of morality. It's true that the oath has no such program, since it is an oath to shared action within the many political rifts that are just beginning to open. But, unlike the far right, what we might think of as the proto-communist oath is not unified by identity but by a reflective fidelity to the unrest itself. It was the universal character of this oath that was able to bring juggalos together with indebted college graduates in Occupy and to unite football hooligans with slum-dwellers in Egypt. The unity of this oath is therefore the inclusive, flowing unity of those who wish to push the rift open, to spread it further, to extend it longer, or to ensure that the potential spreads. Instead of an oath of blood, it is therefore an oath of water, the "party of Anarchy" that seems to seek nothing but further erosion, the growth of the flood.

The oath of blood is an oath of exclusive unity, in which action is taken on behalf of a "community" to be defended or actualized. It is therefore easy for those beholden to this oath to sever themselves from the dynamics of the crowd and even to abhor mass unrest as such, seeing in it only the rise of an undifferentiated

mob or rabble capable of nothing but degenerative chaos.
The oath of blood reaches its apex, then, in militia- or gang-like
minority groupings of the type described by Kilcullen. These
groupings will seek to build local, communitarian spheres as
part of a drive to "start the world" in the midst of the material
community of capital's widespread social decay. In contrast,
the oath of water is an oath of inclusive unity, in which action
is inherently partisan action taken alongside and on behalf of
the crowd, dependent on constant expansion. When severed
from the mass momentum of the historical party, those beholden
to this oath cannot properly act in its name. There is no true
"autonomy" from the material community of capital, only fidelity
to its destruction.

Fucked Generations

In Hong Kong, defeat came like the rain. First the gangsters
attacked in isolated downpours on behalf of the government,
weakening morale in the already late stages of a stagnating
movement. Then torrents of police overtook the barricades at
their weakest points, targeting the strongest occupation (in Mong
Kok), after the others had fallen. In Seattle, defeat also came like
the rain. After the camp moved from downtown to Capitol Hill,
it was slowly ground down. Shuffling through the mud between
rain-soaked tents, the moment at which it all collapsed could
hardly be identified, but that defeat was clear. The homeless had
slowly filled the camp as others left and the minimal services
provided had begun to atrophy. Here the police never came in
torrents. They just hovered around the camp in small groups,
like a light, drizzling mist that slowly soaked through everything
until no one was quite sure who was a plainclothes cop and
who wasn't. The community college used the presence of the
homeless as an excuse to finally evict the occupation, complaining
of open-air drug use and harassment of female students. The

police never even had to clear the camp. At the end of one of the longest-lasting Occupations in the country, people ultimately just packed up and left.

Whether the rain is torrential or perpetual, both Occupations found themselves confronted with cities that were built as little more than sluices for water and capital. Westlake, Mong Kok, Zuccotti Park: these are areas behind the palace walls, yet somehow below the conference rooms and executive suites that helm global circulation. And circulation is one key to this riddle. As Joshua Clover has argued, our era of riots is not unprecedented, but instead corresponds to long global economic cycles in which production and circulation alternate in their centrality. In eras when production dominates, the strike becomes the primary weapon of proletarians because the productive upswing tends to push more people into the industrial workforce, bringing them into direct contact with the immediate process of production and thereby making it possible to halt this process through a refusal to work. In periods such as our own, when circulation dominates and people are forced outside the immediate process of production, things like riots, occupations, and blockades rise to the forefront of global unrest, all defined by their attempt to attack the economy's circulatory system—in the form of blockaded highways and ports or attempts to occupy and thereby disrupt centers of commerce, such as Wall Street in New York or Central in Hong Kong.[30]

Clover also offers a social anatomy of recent unrest, which is marked by a "double riot," in which the indebted, overeducated graduate with no future finds herself unified with those more entirely excluded from the economy in the course of the Long Crisis. This is not some sort of overlap of simple sociological categories, however, since the two dimensions of the double riot are really just two faces of the same global surplus: "The explosive growth of the indebted sector is another face of informalization in which finance capital's need to find debtors dovetails with the explosion of populations driven below subsistence wages."[31] In many instances, the social base of recent conflagrations has quickly extended beyond just these two key demographics, as should be the goal of any truly expansive political event. But in almost all instances, one or both of these social strata seem to be the necessary kindling.

In part, this is because both sides of the "double riot" have a sort of bare exposure to circulation that other demographics do not. While the secular decline in the rate of economic growth has meant that surplus characteristics are more generally distributed across the population, they are not distributed equally. Many of those who are materially within the surplus population in some way (most often as completely superfluous service workers in some arcane insurance, healthcare, or education bureaucracy) nonetheless retain stronger forms of insulation from the immis-erating effects of economic stagnation. This insulation takes the form of selective holdovers from the last economic boom: things like access to affordable health insurance, consistent credit, a viable mortgage, the ability to claim bankruptcy on one's debts, and social security eligibility and other retirement benefits. Taken together, these features ensure that some strata of the population retain strong access to the market despite both the relative super-fluity of their employment and the insufficiency of their direct wage income.

The Marxist economist Andrew Kliman has even gone so far as to argue, somewhat controversially, that the total combination of non-wage benefits u.s. companies offer to workers, when calcu-lated as part of their wage, completely eliminates the appearance of overall wage decline or stagnation for the American working class as a whole.[32] Instead of across-the-board wage loss, there is a series of new polarizations within the class, the most important of which is the split between those with salaries and benefits, and those subsisting purely on wages.[33] Rather than corporations gaining profits at the expense of workers, then, Kliman argues that "although the typical worker's share fell to some degree, what actually rose at his or her expense was the share of the income distributed to more highly paid employees."[34]

The racial dynamics of this divide have been widely demonstrated, and are most salient in the disparity in subprime foreclosures after the burst of the housing bubble. But the particular ways that this polarization breaks down according to age are often less emphasized, though arguably more important since they span racial groups, aggravate already existing racial inequities, and perfectly match the J-Curve model of rising expectations reaching a sudden reversal, leading to widespread discontent. This generational dimension is also deceptively fundamental to understanding class and crisis for the simple fact that class does not return to the forefront of politics as soon as crisis breaks out. The return of class is instead part of the unfolding of the Long Crisis over time. As class conflict intensifies, the traditional methods of separation and sequestration of struggles— as "issues" concerning particular "communities" or "interest groups"—will tend to strain and then shatter.

This dispossession occurs across decades. The sphere of those who are insulated from the crisis shrinks, though white baby boomers remain at its core as the demographic who most benefited from the last golden age. In part, this shrinkage entails the pushing-out of the less fortunate, never fully included blue-collar members of their coddled generation—a phenomenon already visible in mortality and morbidity rates among the poorest strata of older whites, the political consequences of which were already examined in previous chapters. But it also occurs through the retirement and subsequent, well-deserved die-off of the elderly. It is this process that will ultimately guarantee a return to more distinct class lines in the future, sketched around new polarities of access to the historically unprecedented mass of wealth flowing through inheritance and all its effects on housing prices, inflation, and taxation. This slow game of class warfare is politically palatable precisely because it does not entail stripping a privileged generation of its benefits all at once. It is substantially easier never to offer things than to take them away.

But as millions of Beatles-loving, Trump-and-Hillary-voting, homeowning baby boomers die off, their particular anti-communist brain-rot dies with them. The generational divide here really does drive down to the most basic level: around the same time that the u.s. had finally imprisoned the same share of its population as the USSR under the height of the gulag system, I remember a baby boomer explaining to me that the most important difference between capitalism and "communism" was that under capitalism the government can't just spy on you, kick down your door, and search your property. A few years later, of course, the government was kicking down my door and searching my property, all because I was identified out of a picture-book of "known anarchists," based on intel gathered by thorough surveillance of my house, local protests, and online social networks. For these people, the urn cannot approach quickly enough.

Tombs

Sometimes I can only remember Occupy as a sort of impressionistic mesh of bodies pushed together and hurled for a moment through a cacophony of echoes: the crowd echoing back its own words, the police grenades echoing off the asphalt, our own chants echoing off the cold glass palaces built for money and the people designated to handle it in lump sums—for a moment these echoes seemed to vibrate something deep down in things, stirring our flesh as if it were a fluid that could never quite be trapped in its entirety, throwing our voices back at us from the steel and glass in a languageless roar as if to invoke the utterly world-breaking, if ultimately fleeting, realization that such palaces could fall. As everything else gave way to work, jail, and simple, grinding time, something of that feeling has nonetheless remained: the vague impression of power, glimpsed for a moment by the first of many proletarian generations to come.

The echoes also hint at how and where that power ran up against insurmountable limits, like a soft, organic thing crashing into a hard wall of granite. Despite all the tactical centrality of small, pragmatic grouplets and the self-absorbed, self-declared leadership of the activists, the reality is that struggles today have a limited range of motion, and most decisions are not really choices between equally valid tactics (or a "diversity of tactics") but simply the path of least resistance that allows the struggle to advance or consigns it to stagnation. In the vast majority of cases, this path of least resistance is strongly determined by geography and wears down rapidly in environments that have been built to be inhospitable to such events. At the same time, the unrest does not simply end, because the large-scale material conditions that summon it have not disappeared. Individual struggles are therefore submitted to a sort of evolutionary meat grinder. The vast majority are dead ends, due to either their environment or their internal incoherence or completely random contingencies or likely some combination of all the above.

Occupy Wall Street, the Movement of the Squares, Occupy Hong Kong, and even earlier, more subdued events such as the 2011 occupation of the Wisconsin State Capitol building were all starved in similar ways. The Invisible Committee, an amorphous global analytic body founded around an obscure group of French communists, describes this predicament with a suitable eloquence:

> when the insurgents manage to penetrate parliaments, presidential palaces, and other headquarters of institutions, as in Ukraine, in Libya or in Wisconsin, it's only to discover empty places, that is, empty of power, and furnished without any taste. It's not to prevent the "people" from "taking power" that they are so fiercely kept from invading such places, but to prevent them from realizing that power no

longer resides in the institutions. There are only deserted
temples there, decommissioned fortresses, nothing but stage
sets—real traps for revolutionaries.[35]

And this argument can be extended beyond their list of political
holograms to include the spectacular centers of circulation and
high-tech production embodied in the downtown core. On the
one hand, the activity of such centers is rarely shut down by these
kinds of protests, since they are confined to the vaguely defined
"public" sphere of parks and boulevards, and thereby exist just
beyond the final wall of the fortress, contained in those cavernous
avenues designed for the easy movement of police tanks and
hordes of tourists. On the other, if such unrest does grow to
sufficient proportions to be capable of disrupting these high-end
services, the riot fails via its very success, finding the skyscrapers
and shopping malls to be little more than deserts once capital
has fled. These are not hospitable places for any sort of struggle
to reproduce itself—they are hardly hospitable to humans
whatsoever. Meanwhile, the executive functions of the global
city are quickly shipped away to other brain hubs, remaining
funds transferred to offshore accounts. The victory of such an
insurrection is its own tomb.

Other than a handful of half-abandoned cities in global rust
belts, the downtown cores of most metropoles in the u.s. are little
more than gigantic, airless coffins built to suffocate such movements in their infancy. This constitutes one of the first major
limits in the early evolutionary chaos that dominates present
struggles. Nonetheless, collision with this limit remains the
path of least resistance, evidenced by the unerring tendency
for protests to gravitate toward simple, largely nonessential
circulatory systems in the urban core. The seemingly natural
response to the late 2014 Grand Jury non-indictment in the
murder of Michael Brown, for example, was for nationwide
solidarity marches to storm freeways, shutting down the flow

of interstate traffic in several major cities, including Los Angeles, Oakland, Seattle, St Louis, Dallas, and Nashville, as well as major bridges in New York and Washington, DC. Aside from a certain symbolic victory, this response met with the same hollow anti-climax as Occupy's attempt to storm the empty corridors of power years earlier. Freeways could not be held for more than a few hours, freight was rerouted, and the ports, factories, and warehouses all kept running as per usual.

At the time, I remember people flooding onto I-5 in Seattle where it dips down and tunnels beneath Freeway Park. Most ran forward into the dimly lit cavern of the express lanes, attempt-ing to catch a glimpse of the front line of police vehicles and the bright storm of headlights behind. Others fled back as the police moved the line forward to make arrests. I stayed in the middle, just walking in the empty, echoing chamber. That insufferable local rapper Macklemore ran by me with a few members of his entourage and a handful of people from the black bloc, all pointing and yelling in the direction of some approaching but unseen contingent of police. In a surreal few moments, we all escaped over the embankment and fled into the winding, modernist maze of Freeway Park, stumbling around homeless people, running into other protestors who came up to shake Macklemore's hand and say something about white privilege. Macklemore's picture would be on the news the next day, his fist raised in the center of the abandoned road. And that image, if anything, is the sum of the present limit of struggle: a celebrity on a blockaded roadway, where spectacle overlaps with peoples' rudimentary grasp of circulation, rather than parliament or the "public," as the present ground for class conflict.

The End

They don't have a Macklemore in Baton Rouge, thank God. But everything echoes. As soon as the shots are fired, we know the repetition well enough to play along: the first round of protests, the promise of justice, the National Guard put on alert, things calming as the slow legal machinery grinds away in the background, paid leave for the shooter, pundits and politicians praising "the dialogue" that has begun. And then the grand jury or the committee or just some fucking chief or judge comes back with the verdict: not even a trial but simply the conclusion that there will not be one, that all was justified. Then there is the second round, like the first, a million rehearsals of a stalled revolution. And by then how many other cities? How many other repetitions? Regardless of the number, each repetition brings a certain change in the valence of struggle. Things mutate. They retreat and advance in increments. But they all have the same soundtrack. If this soundtrack could be reduced to its purest form, it would probably just be the sound of guns cocking over an infinite progression of trap snares, and maybe a vocal track with Young Thug at his most incoherent. But in its concrete form, it is an anthem.

In Ferguson, I watched as someone dragged a loudspeaker from a nearby car out into the street directly across from a line of police, plugged in some shitty cell phone with an aux cord, and then held the phone up toward the line of cops as if it was a dead man's switch. His head hooded, eyes utterly placid, he pushed the button and the police moved forward almost immediately, like automatons activated by the same mechanism. Lil Boosie's "Fuck the Police" blasted out of the speaker directly toward the police. The song spun into the crowd and seemed to push it forward. Despite their absolute numerical advantage, the police moved faster, sensing the precipice, as if the track could simply not be allowed to complete—like some sort of ancient incantation begun by this young hooded black man on the humid, moonlit streets of Missouri and all of us in the crowd now disciples of it, drawn toward the song as if we were circling the event horizon of a black hole sunk in the middle of Florissant. The police were there before the first verses had ended. They ripped the aux cord from the speaker with a loud pop and forced the hooded youth onto his knees.

The song was by a Baton Rouge rapper sentenced in one of America's harshest state penal systems to eight years for drug charges, the bulk of which involved simple marijuana possession.[36] The events in Ferguson broke out only months after his early release. Boosie had served roughly five years in Louisiana State Penitentiary some 50 miles from Baton Rouge in Angola, a notorious prison often likened to a modern-day slave plantation.[37] Several months after his release and two months after his song had become a new national anthem in Ferguson, he changed his name from Lil Boosie to Boosie Badazz. The song would continue to be played in later protests, until two years later everything seemed to come full circle when another black man, Alton Sterling, was shot to death by the police point blank in Boosie's hometown.

In some slow, imperceptible way, the storms above St Louis had flooded into the rivers and the aquifers and the slow grind of that ancient river had washed it all southward with a vast, writhing indifference. But when it emerged in this new climate, the unrest had changed somehow. On these southern shores, the repetitions suddenly seemed to be amplified, everything echoing everything else. Baton Rouge is a decentralized city on the banks of the Mississippi, a sprawling New South sister to Rust Belt St Louis. It helms the tenth largest port in the u.s. (by tonnage shipped)[38] and sits at the center of the region's petrochemical and manufacturing industries. This also places it at the northern end of Louisiana's notorious Cancer Alley. When the protests came to Baton Rouge, the police were no longer concerned with simply forcing people to march in circles and stay off public streets. With little in the way of public space in the sprawling near hinterland, they instead chased protestors onto people's lawns, making mass arrests, flanked by armored vehicles emitting painful acoustic blasts designed for crowd control.[39] And the crowd seemed to have changed as well. Police had their teeth knocked out, and guns were reportedly confiscated from protestors.[40] Despite attempts by activists to focus the protests on City Hall, they quickly spilled out into the surrounding residential area, embedding the protests within neighborhoods, rather than sealing it off in the empty corridors of downtown.

The sequence was cut short when a man named Gavin Long shot six police officers in a targeted attack, following a pattern already established by Micah Johnson in Dallas ten days earlier. The same conditions that prevent political cohesion within the tomb of the downtown core amplify the already-extreme atomization of the material community of capital, each defeat seeming to isolate its sympathizers even more, the sequence of failures first like waves of rubble deposited on top of you and then like great, crushing strata of stone. The very inescapability of a world with "no alternative" generates an isolating pressure that hardens those already lost, condensing any remaining hope down into a diamond-sharp hatred of the world in its entirety. Though in essence a far-right phenomenon, the lone wolf often simultaneously lays claim to right-wing and left-wing discourse, fusing the two together in a spectacular but otherwise incoherent reduction of politics to a single moment of sublime violence.

The lone wolf has no politics. For him (and they are almost exclusively male), left and right collapse into the pure act, the sovereignty of the individual will. Whether targeting the correct enemy (police, the rich) or a scapegoated one (immigrants, Muslims, black people), there is no revolutionary thrust to the act other than a vague expectation that the spectacle might by the slimmest chance inspire some sort of larger break in the status quo—that people might finally see the ostensibly unseen operation of power, or that the sleeping might become "woke." In a way, these conspiracy-theorist, sovereign citizen mass murderers are less respectable than their purely apolitical cop-killer counterparts—the ones who are simply in it for mild revenge and simple mathematics, figuring that as long as they take out more than one cop, the world will be a better place, on balance. With no other perceptible options, the lone wolf proclaims that he has become a vanguard-unto-himself and performs the only action that seems possible. Founded on absolute exclusion, this is the oath of blood metastasized until it is nothing but an oath to pure, salvific action, exonerated of all commitments and worthy of judgment only according to an utterly abstracted ethics of fidelity.

But despite its dampening effect, the unrest in Baton Rouge was not ended by Long's actions alone. The following months brought not only a wave of extreme police repression but historical flooding in Louisiana, at first largely ignored by the media despite being the worst natural disaster since Hurricane Sandy in 2012. One interview with a participant in the Baton Rouge protests notes the significance of this sequence:

> In a broader sense, it's also worth noting that in quick secession [sic], a large American population just experienced firsthand three of the most paradigmatic phenomena of our times: an anti-police uprising, a mass-shooting, and a climate-related catastrophe. Taken together we have a neat diorama of the existential disaster capitalism has thrown us into.[41]

It's worth wondering what might have happened had this sequence been reversed, with a mass uprising occurring in the wake of environmental destruction and a lone wolf attack against the police. The confluence of events here begins to open unseen possibilities, as ultras from new rounds of riots might operate within a scene of massive environmental devastation and the extreme polarization caused by anti-police attacks.

Though it is yet to be seen how such struggles might mutate in the future, we are now approaching a point at which the expanding unrest of the Long Crisis is beginning to overlap more directly with the geography of the near hinterland, which will soon become its center of gravity. After yet another police shooting in Charlotte, North Carolina, protestors not only blocked the interstate (I-85), but began looting container trucks and setting the contents on fire. Such events hint that our era's constellation of constantly sparking and dimming riots, occupations, and blockades is thereby on a slow collision course with the mainline of the global economy. This coincidence between a more hospitable environment and constantly innovating waves of unrest is likely to begin to provide (over the next five, ten, or fifteen years) the rudiments of some sort of adaptation capable of overcoming the present limits of the riot. Baton Rouge provides one window into what this might look like, laid out first in reverse.

The Coming Flood

In Egypt, the early sequence of demonstrations, strikes, and small-scale riots was transformed into an insurrection only by the intervention of small, competent tactical teams who fused with the crowd and demonstrated a degree of strength in the face of a seemingly unshakeable regime. On the streets, the key battles that turned the movement into a genuine insurrection were led by football Ultras—first in the successful battle for Qasr al-Nil Bridge on January 28, and then in the "Battle of the Camels" six days later, in which Ultras (now joined by the youth wing of the Muslim Brotherhood) led the demonstrators in fighting off regime-backed militias and gangs of hired thugs bused in from outside the city. In the digital realm, the soft war counterpart to the street war below was led by similarly small tactical groupings of hackers (some from Egypt, but many operating elsewhere) who were able to breach the communications lockdown imposed by the regime—a key element in spreading the news of the uprising across Egypt and abroad. Similarly, after the police were defeated and the demonstrations had evolved into a full-scale uprising, many districts in Cairo fell into the control of local, anti-regime "citizens' committees" and neighborhood watch groups, many members of which had not participated in the uprising itself but now sought to help sustain it. By building strength in an environment of competitive control, all of these small groups had helped to amplify the conflict, extend it to new territories and drive its roots deeper into society.[42]

The actions of lone wolf attackers, absent any collective dimension, cannot lead to such amplification, since they are fundamentally symptomatic figures. But small, capable groups of ultras, even if ad hoc ones, clearly can create such an amplification, given the right conditions and the ability to demonstrate a certain degree of strength in street wars, digital conflicts, and social reproduction within liberated territories. It's also via these small groupings that adaptations capable of overcoming the riot can take hold, and future organizational potentials can be dimly glimpsed, since their fidelity to the unrest itself is capable of carrying over after the immediate window of the riot has closed—the historical party gives birth to many formal parties that may play important roles in future sequences of unrest. The ultras, then, are a sort of vanguard for the historical party, not in the sense that they lead its advances or helm it ideologically, but in the sense that they represent the forefront of mutation and adaptation in the evolutionary meat grinder of global struggles.

This is where the question of the Baton Rouge sequence in reverse might offer a potential window to the future, the floods of 2016 foreboding a greater flood stirring in those aquifers buried deep beneath St Louis, beneath Baton Rouge, and beneath even the inhuman body of the Mississippi, that great engine of destruction cast in the shape of a river. In an atmosphere of deep pro-regime/anti-regime polarization, on a chaotic terrain isolated by natural disaster, what shape might a mass uprising take and how might small groupings of ultras operate to advance it? Such an event is most likely to take place in capital's near hinterland, where population is increasing alongside immiseration, and power has not yet adapted to the threats arising beyond the palace walls. In a way, this is an impossible question to answer. The process is fundamentally evolutionary, and any overcoming of the limits of the riot remains unknown. But the conditions in which this overcoming takes place can be roughly predicted.

As the Long Crisis continues, the hinterland grows and peri-urban zones undergo the harshest forms of stratification. White poverty deepens alongside an influx of new migrants and the displacement of inner-city poverty into the suburbs. There are very few areas that might be able to guarantee some sort of general social safety net to their urban fringe, and even where such guarantees might emerge, they will be contingent on the rapidly shifting predilections of finance capital. Meanwhile, the urban fringe in many places will move inward, especially when the next bubbles burst and the gains of the tech industry are shown to be hollow. In general, then, those within the hinterland will increasingly be thrown into a condition of survival on the edge of the wage relation, mirrored by their sequestration at the geographic edge of the city or within the vast catchment of the abandoned Rust Belt core. Survival here will take many forms, and is certain to depend on intricate methods of second- and third-hand profiting off various state bureaucracies as corruption and credit fill the holes left by a receding tide of formal employment. All of this will be thrown disproportionately on the shoulders of younger generations.

This will raise the question of reproduction for future struggles in these zones—such as the citizens' committees and neighborhood watches organized in Cairo. Such questions were already hinted at during Occupy, with its communal kitchens, trash-disposal working groups, and even attempts at voluntary, free provisions for basic healthcare. But in each instance, these communal footholds were founded on inhospitable terrain, forced to use all their effort not to be scrubbed off the concrete by police or Parks and Recreation crews sent to keep the downtown core clean of such nuisances (which, it might be noted, don't fulfill any unmet needs for most of downtown's residents, with the notable exception of the homeless). In the hinterland, by contrast, most oppositional forces are poorly organized, and the population is often actually in need of such services, particularly in times of ecological disaster. Service programs—suitable for the present but roughly analogous to the Black Panthers' breakfast program, the iww's (Industrial Worker's of the World) housing of itinerant laborers, or the social clubs of the early workers' movement—are likely to be an essential component of any attempt to overcome the present limits of struggle in the u.s., as are emergency pre-paredness courses such as those offered by the Oath Keepers and disaster relief services like those run by church groups in the wake of the floods.

At the same time, the intricate ways in which exclusion from the wage forces proletarians into vicious, predatory behavior for survival also ensures that the expanding bulk of corrupt bureau-cracy will cleave such neighborhoods into warring parties, dividing them along lines of predation disguised as order on one side and abjection disguised as simple criminality or moral failure on the other. As in Ferguson, we will see local solutions to the problem of austerity that take the form of extra-tax fees, fines, and simple expropriations of the worse-off populations within crisis-stricken cities. In Egypt, those deeply dependent on the corrupt govern-ment were the ones who staffed the pro-regime militias, while others were simply paid lump sums and bused in from the exurbs to fight on the conservatives' side in the Battle of the Camels. In some instances, the expansion of such corruption in the u.s. will still be public in character, enforced by the local police, feeding into the courts, and funneling cash into a number of other arms of local government that may appear to have nothing to do with such corruption yet nonetheless depend on it for their sources of funding—the welfare of the elementary school teacher here alloyed with that of the police. In other instances, such corruption might take on a more private shape, whether in the form of local criminal syndicates, scam artists, or loan sharks.

In most places, the center has already fallen. Liberalism offers no solution, and the new rents of the near hinterland begin to determine new political polarities, just as access to federal money determines politics in the countryside. There are those who collect the fines, and those who pay them. In Baton Rouge, the geography of this stratification is particularly clear, with opposing poles of the near hinterland warring against one another:

> As capitol [sic] of Louisiana, Baton Rouge and the neighboring parishes are home to a lot of the state's most racist populations whose sentiments played a big part in passing America's first Blue Lives Matter Bill back in May, which makes targeting police a hate crime.

> Nearly half of the BRPD itself is manned by residents of neighboring Livingston Parish, an overwhelmingly white area known in the recent past for KKK activity. Even the cops who actually live in Baton Rouge Parish are mostly from the white neighborhoods.[43]

This is the geography of latent civil war, the interests of the wealthy downtown core aligned with its extremities in the form of the militarized white exurb, a recruiting hub for the far right. Any evolution of the riot in these conditions will be defined by how it manages this polarity. The state will almost certainly ship in Klansmen from the exurbs or simply recruit angry whites with the promise of painkillers, just as Mubarak bused in scimitar-wielding conservatives from the countryside to lead gangs of poor men paid in free meals and Tramadol.

In such a situation, the correctness of one's political analysis is irrelevant.

Far-right solutions—even spectacular ones that might glory in some success over parliamentarians or armed federal agents—will tend in the final instance to fuse with the predatory party in this civil war, as is obvious in the case of groups such as Golden Dawn in Greece, bolstered by the votes and donations of police, civil servants, and nativist workers. Communist, or at least proto-communist, potentials will exhibit the opposite tendency, advocating an inclusive allegiance with the abject, including poor whites, and the absolute rejection of any "community" that denies such universalism.

The far right is currently based in the hinterland's white exurbs, finding in these neighborhoods a pragmatic border between the poverty of the far hinterland and the predatory flow of income drawn from the city and the near hinterland. These "small town" exurbs often play an equally central role in the ideology of the far right, as its community in microcosm—all despite the fact that such neighborhoods are entirely dependent on their economic links with the downtown core. The liberal residents of the city proper are, meanwhile, able to build political legitimacy by disavowing these right-wing hubs while still depending on them for the security of the palace walls. All of this reinforces the warrior mythology of the far right, which sees itself as a form of bitter but necessary barbarity mobilized against the greater barbarity of the proletarian horde (of which they are just one disavowed fragment).

There are at least two identifiable dimensions, then, to the future overcoming of the riot. There is first the intensive dimension, defined by questions of provision and reproduction, and, second, the extensive one, defined by latent civil war. But both dimensions exist within the larger framework of national states and global production. Extensively, the near hinterland is particularly important, since future struggles on such sites have

the capacity to fundamentally cripple global supply chains
in a way that the occupation of parliaments or parks in front
of financial centers simply do not. Again, these conditions are
best visualized in the sprawling Sunbelt: "the L.A. region is
currently the largest manufacturing hub in the United States,"
even while "two of the three major metro statistical areas present
in Southern California accounted for the 3rd (I.E. [Inland Empire])
and 6th (L.A.) highest unemployment rates in the country in terms
of regions with over one million inhabitants."[44] A central Pacific
Rim manufacturing hub, integral to global production, thereby
exists directly alongside one of the country's greatest concentrations of the unemployed, sequestered in logistics cities on the
urban fringe:

> This concentrated conflation, between carceral surplus
> populations and capitalist functionaries, is mirrored in the
> fortified infrastructure of Southern California's logistics
> networks. Commodity-capital flows, with cargo throughput
> reaching millions of dollars per day, pulse through the
> below ground-level trench of the Alameda Corridor (while
> hidden from view) through the very dispossessed South
> LA communities that many of those incarcerated in the
> MDC [Metropolitan Detention Center] come from.[45]

It is this neighbored concentration of industry and dispossession
that opens new extensive horizons for struggles as they evolve
past the riot, giving them the ability to spread disruption beyond
their local sphere in a way not dependent on media spectacle.

A number of theories have arisen to try and account for how
these features might be combined in some speculative future
evolution of current struggles. Clover condenses a number of
loosely fitting theories about "communization" into a clear
argument for "the commune," defined by its ability to facilitate
self-reproduction while also "absolutizing" the antagonism of

the riot. The Invisible Committee offers fleeting glimpses of something similar, though too shrouded in smoke and flowery French prose to be entirely visible from our present vantage point. Many anarchists offer yet another sketch, founded this time on an "autonomy" that tends to conflate small-scale moments of self-reproduction in squats and occupations with the nationalist or proto-nationalist enclaves of populist movements in the global countryside. Frederic Jameson, meanwhile, represents a popular strain of academic Marxism in opting for the older language of "dual power," founding the reproductive and extensive capacity of future struggles on the reinvented institution of the "universal army."[46] Despite their myriad shortcomings and many different vocabularies, all of these theories share the recognition that the evolution of the riot is a process of building power within the interstices opened by the Long Crisis.

Personally, I don't understand the compulsion to mine history for words that might describe what's to come. The fact is that the approaching flood has no name. Any title it might take is presently lost in the noise of its gestation, maybe just beginning to be spoken in a language that we can hardly recognize. There will be no Commune because this isn't Paris in 1871. There will be no Dual Power because this isn't Russia in 1917. There will be no Autonomy because this isn't Italy in 1977. I'm writing this in 2017, and I don't know what's coming, even though I know something is rolling toward us in the darkness, and the world can end in more ways than one. Its presence is hinted at somewhere deep inside the evolutionary meat grinder of riot repeating riot, all echoing ad infinitum through the Year of our Lord 2016, when the anthem returned to its origin, and the corpse flowers bloomed all at once as Louisiana was turned to water, and no one knew why. I don't call people comrade; I just call them friend. Because whatever's coming has no name, and anyone who says they hear it is a liar. All I hear are guns cocking over trap snares unrolling to infinity.

References

Introduction

1 For more on the concept, see the work of Peter K. Haff, in particular, "Technology as a Geological Phenomenon: Implications for Human Well-being," *Geological Society, London*, Special Publications 395, no. 1 (2014), pp. 301–9.

2 This number is almost certainly an underestimate, due to China's household registration (*hukou*) system, in which migrant workers are not officially counted as urbanites, since they are still registered in their home villages. Many Chinese statistics now provide surveys and estimates of this additional urban population, but the true number is probably far greater; "China Urbanization Rate Reached 56% in 2015," CCTV, http://english.cntv.com, accessed February 12, 2017.

3 'World's Population Increasingly Urban with More than Half Living in Urban Areas," United Nations (July 10, 2014).

4 See Saskia Sassen, *The Global City: New York, London, Tokyo* (Princeton, NJ, 1991).

5 Richard Florida, "The 25 Most Economically Powerful Cities in the World," www.citylab.com (September 15, 2011); Richard Florida, "If U.S. Cities were Countries, How Would They Rank?", www.theatlantic.com (July 21, 2011).

6 Richard Florida, *The Rise of the Creative Class: And How It's Transforming Work, Leisure, Community and Everyday Life* (New York, 2002).

7 Enrico Moretti, *The New Geography of Jobs* (New York, 2012), p. 5.

8 Aaron Benanav, "Precarity Rising," *Viewpoint Magazine* (June 15, 2015).

9 Ibid.

10 Robert J. Gordon, *The Rise and Fall of American Growth: The U.S. Standard of Living Since the Civil War* (Princeton, NJ, 2016), p. 3.

11 Ibid., p. 14, figs 1–2.

12 Ibid., p. 17.

13 Ibid., p. 22.

14 For an overview of these trends in China, see "No Way Forward, No Way Back: China in the Era of Riots," *Chuang*, 1: Dead Generations (Oakland, CA, 2016), www.chuangcn.org.

15 Aaron Benanav and *Endnotes*, "Misery and Debt," *Endnotes*, 2 (Glasgow, 2010).

16 Saskia Sassen, *Expulsions: Brutality and Complexity in the Global Economy* (Cambridge, 2014), p. 31.

17 Kathryn J. Edin and H. Luke Shaefer, *$2.00 A Day: Living on Almost Nothing in America* (Boston, MA, 2016), p. XVII. The number here is almost certainly a conservative underestimate, and the trend appears to have either increased or plateaued in recent years. For more on the data used and more recent estimates, see Kathryn J. Edin and H. Luke Shaefer, "What is the Evidence of Worsening Conditions among America's Poorest Families with Children?" www.twodollarsaday.com, accessed February 20, 2017.

18 See *Endnotes*, "A History of Separation," *Endnotes*, 4 (Glasgow, 2015).

1 Oaths of Blood

1 The "Third Position" comes from the old right-wing claim to be "beyond left and right," and today generally refers to an array of groups who merge right-wing and left-wing elements in novel combinations that make it hard to identify the far right thrust of their politics. Among the most successful are Casa Pound in Italy; the extremist wing of the Yellow Shirts in Thailand, with its core among the Buddhist fundamentalist group Santi Asoke; and an array of Ukrainian national anarchist and neo-fascist groups that rose to prominence during Euromaidan. For more on this global phenomenon, see NPC, "The Solstice: On the Rise of the Right-wing Mass Movements, Winter 2013/2014," Ultra, www.ultra-com.org, April 27, 2014.

2 For an overview of the Wolves of Vinland, see Betsy Woodruff, "Inside Virginia's Creepy White-power Wolf Cult," The Daily Beast, www.thedailybeast.com, November 11, 2015.

3 Donovan has written a number of books with titles such as *The Way of Men* and *Becoming a Barbarian*; he also runs an eponymous blog, in which he regularly profiles the activities of the Wolves and similar groups.

4 At the same time, connection to the more traditionally racist thrust of white nationalism is by no means absent. One of their active Virginia members, Maurice Michaely, spent time in prison for burning down a black church, and much of the support for their early projects came from traditional white nationalist groups.

5 Jack Donovan, "A Time for Wolves," www.jackdonovan.com, June 2014.

6   Qtd. in Woodruff, "Inside Virginia's Creepy White-power Wolf Cult."

7   "The Oath Keepers: Anti-government Extremists Recruiting Military and Police," Anti-defamation League, www.adl.org, September 16, 2015.

8   For a detailed look at one such border-op, see Shane Bauer, "Undercover with a Border Militia," *Mother Jones*, www.motherjones.com, November/December 2016.

9   David Neiwert, "III Percenters' Ride Wave of Islamophobia in Idaho to Lead Anti-refugee Protests," Southern Poverty Law Center, www.splcenter.org, November 4, 2015.

10 There is a substantial Basque population in Northern Nevada and Southern Idaho, part of the global Basque diaspora. Most originally migrated during the Gold Rush and went on to work as shepherds during the grazing season. Many towns in the area have visible Basque architecture and host annual Basque festivals.

11 Byard Duncan, "In the Rural West, Residents Choose Low Taxes over Law Enforcement," Reveal News, www.revealnews.org, June 2, 2016.

12 Spencer Sunshine, Jessica Campbell, Daniel HoSang, Steven Besa, and Chip Berlet, "Up in Arms: A Guide to Oregon's Patriot Movement," *Rural Organizing Project*, 2016, p. 11, available at www.rop.org/up-in-arms/.

13 Tay Wiles, "Sugar Pine Mine, the Other Standoff," High Country News, www.hcn.org, February 2, 2016.

14 "The Oath Keepers Are Ready for War with the Federal Government," *Vice*, www.vice.com, September 14, 2015.

15 "They Are the Oath Keepers, We Are the Peace Makers," Rural Organizing Project, www.rop.org, May 7, 2015.

16 David Kilcullen, *Out of the Mountains: The Coming Age of the Urban Guerrilla* (New York, 2013), p. 126.

17 Rent is used here in its more expansive definition drawn from Marxist economics, which includes taxation, interest paid on debt, land rent, and all forms of simple extortion.

18 Carol Hardy Vincent, Laura A. Hanson, and Jerome P. Bjelopera, "Federal Land Ownership: Overview and Data," Congressional Research Service, December 29, 2014, p. 1.

19 Ibid., p. 7, Table 1.

20 Andrew McColl, "The Massive, Empty Federal Lands of the American West," *The Atlantic*, www.theatlantic.com, January 5, 2016.

21 For a good history of the phenomenon, see Steven C. Beda, "Landscapes of Solidarity: Timber Workers and the Making of Place in the Pacific Northwest, 1900–1964," PhD Diss., University of Washington (2014).

22 I haven't been able to verify these exact numbers, but it is notable that the right-wing think tank the Property and Environment Research Center calculated roughly the same proportional difference

in the two agencies in a report designed to emphasize the opposite point, arguing that state management returned higher revenues than federal. See Holly Fretwell and Shawn Regan, "Divided Lands: State vs. Federal Management in the West," The Property and Environment Research Center, www.perc.org, 2015.

23 Table DP03, "Selected Economic Characteristics" for Burns city, Oregon, 2010–2014 American Community Survey 5-Year Estimates.

24 Table DP03, "Selected Economic Characteristics" for Harney County, Oregon, 2010–2014 American Community Survey 5-Year Estimates.

25 There is at least rudimentary evidence, at the time of writing, that this population provided an essential support base for Trump in the 2016 election. See Michael A. McCarthy, "The Revenge of Joe the Plumber," Jacobin, www.jacobinmag.com, October 26, 2016.

26 This is an observation of present dynamics, not an absolute fact, and it appears to be a phenomenon contingent on both national history and the incredibly recent rebirth of an earnestly insurrectionary left. In fact, in countries such as Greece, which has suffered for years under the extremities of the crisis, the far right and far left appear much more evenly matched.

27 Crispian Balmer, "Trump's Triumph Puts Italy's Renzi in a Difficult Position," Reuters, www.reuters.com, November 9, 2016.

2 Silver and Ash

1 Jeff Mapes, "Charting the Decline of Oregon's Timber Industry," The Oregonian, www.oregonlive.com, January 23, 2012.

2 Nathanael Johnson, "What One Farmer Learned from Surviving the '80s Farm Crisis," Grist, www.grist.org, April 21, 2015.

3 For the decline in Christianity across the general population, see "America's Changing Religious Landscape," Pew Research Study, www.pewforum.org, May 12, 2015.

4 George Lavender, "Fighting Fires is Big Business for Private Companies," Earth Island Journal, www.earthisland.org, October 29, 2013.

5 "The Rising Cost of Wildfire Operations: Effects on the Forest Service's Non-fire Work," United States Department of Agriculture, www.fs.fed.us, August 4, 2015, pp. 4 and 7.

6 For examples of ex-military contractors, see the Veterans Fire Corps: www.veteransfirecorps.org; for details on the Forest Service's military partnerships, see the agency's own description: "Military Partners," U.S. Forest Service, www.fs.fed.us/fire/partners/military.

7 "Rural America at a Glance, 2016 Edition," United States Department of Agriculture, 2016.

8 Lennon Bergland, "Fighting Wildfires in Western Idaho," Vice, www.vice.com, January 6, 2013.

9 Julia Lurie, "30 Percent of California's Forest Firefighters Are Prisoners," *Mother Jones*, www.motherjones.com, August 14, 2015.

10 Bergland, "Fighting Wildfires in Western Idaho."

11 By far the best book detailing the region is David Rains Wallace, *The Klamath Knot: Explorations of Myth and Evolution* (San Francisco, CA, 1983).

12 Table DPO3, "Selected Economic Characteristics," computed for All Counties Within United States, *5-Year American Community Survey*, 2015.

13 "Poverty Demographics," United States Department of Agriculture Economic Research Service, www.ers.usda.gov, 2014.

14 Ibid.

15 For one study of the rise of such "New Destinations", see Helen Marrow, *New Destination Dreaming: Immigration, Race, and Legal Status in the American South* (Redwood City, CA, 2011).

16 Andrew Schaefer and Beth Mattingly, "Demographic and Economic Characteristics of Immigrant and Native-born Populations in Rural and Urban Places," Carsey School of Public Policy, October 6, 2016, pp. 3–5.

17 Ibid., p. 1.

18 Trevor Logan and John Parman, "The National Rise in Residential Segregation," NBER *Working Paper No. 20934*, National Bureau of Economic Research, February 2015.

19 Daniel T. Lichter, Domineco Parisi, Steven Michael Grice, and Michael C. Taquino, "National Estimates of Racial Segregation in Rural and Small-town America," *Demography*, XLIV/3 (August 2007), pp. 563–81.

20 Daniel T. Lichter, Domenico Parisi, and Michael C. Taquino, "Emerging Patterns of Hispanic Residential Segregation: Lessons from Rural and Small-town America," *Rural Sociology*, LXXI/4 (December 2016), pp. 483–518.

21 "Rural Research Brief," Housing Assistance Council, April 2012.

22 Blood quantum laws are systems used by Native American tribal authorities in the U.S. to define inclusion within the tribe, usually measured by counting back through a family tree and dividing out non-tribal ancestors; it's derived from explicitly racist colonial administrative mechanisms. See https://en.wikipedia.org, accessed October 6, 2017.

23 Pot raids in the area are conducted by the DEA, county taskforces, or, increasingly, private security firms such as LEAR Asset Management Corp., and in recent years have increasingly been justified in terms of environmental protection and drought prevention. For a description of the role played by private paramlitaries, see Max Cherney, "Paramilitaries Are Eradicating California's Illegal Marijuana Grows," Vice News, https://news.vice.com, September 30, 2014.

24 Though illustrated here anecdotally, the phenomenon is backed up by several more wide-ranging studies of rural America, the most

comprehensive of which is available here: Elaine L. Edgcomb and Tamra Thetford, "The Informal Economy: Making it in Rural America," FIELD (2004).

25 Taylor Barnes, "America's 'Shadow Economy' Is Bigger than You Think—and Growing," *Christian Science Monitor*, www.csmonitor. com, November 12, 2009.

26 Eric Bailey, "Pot is Called Biggest Cash Crop," *Los Angeles Times*, www.latimes.com, December 18, 2006.

27 Nick Reding, *Methland: The Death and Life of an American Small Town* (London, 2009).

28 Haeyoun Park and Matthew Bloch, "How the Epidemic of Drug Overdose Deaths Ripples Across America," *New York Times*, www.nytimes.com, January 19, 2016.

29 George T. Díaz, *Border Contraband: A History of Smuggling across the Rio Grande* (Austin, TX, 2015).

30 Edgcomb and Thetfort, "The Informal Economy," pp. 21–4.

31 "Rural America at a Glance," pp. 3 and 5.

32 Mark Muro and Sifan Liu, "Another Clinton-Trump Divide: High-output America vs. Low-output America," The Brookings Institute, www.brookings.edu, November 29, 2016.

33 This is essentially just a restatement of James C. Davies's "J-Curve" theory of revolution. See James C. Davies, "Toward a Theory of Revolution," *American Sociological Review*, XXVII/1 (February 1962), pp. 5–19.

34 "Poverty Rate by Race/Ethnicity," Kaiser Family Foundation, www.kff.org, 2016. (Data collected from the March 2016 Current Population Survey: Annual Social and Economic Supplements.)

35 Josh Keller and Adam Pearce. "This Small Indiana County Sends More People to Prison than San Francisco and Durham N.C., Combined. Why?" *New York Times*, www.nytimes.com, September 2, 2016.

36 Keith Humphreys, "There's Been a Big Decline in the Black Incarceration Rate, and Almost Nobody's Paying Attention," *Washington Post*, www.washingtonpost.com, February 10, 2016.

37 Kristine Phillips, "Drugs Are Killing so Many People in Ohio that Cold-storage Trailers Are Being Used as Morgues," *Washington Post*, www.washingtonpost.com, March 26, 2017.

38 Haeyoun Park and Matthew Bloch, "How the Epidemic of Drug Overdose Deaths Ripples Across America," *New York Times*, www.nytimes.com, January 19, 2016.

39 Joel Achenbach and Dan Keating, "A New Divide in American Death," *Washington Post*, www.thewashingtonpost.com, April 10, 2016.

40 Ibid.

41 Betsy McKay, "Death Rates Rise for Wide Swath of White Adults, Study Finds," *Wall Street Journal*, www.wsj.com, March 23, 2017.

42 Ibid.

43 Achenbach and Keating, "A New Divide in American Death."

44 Chris Wilson, "This Map Shows the Deadliest Counties in the u.s.," *Time*, www.time.com, March 25, 2015.

45 See, for example, this article by an ex-militia member, sparked by a conversation with his Pakistani neighbor: "A Message to the Patriot Movement," Redneck Revolt, www.redneckrevolt.org, February 20, 2017.

46 This refusal is by no means universal, and many white rural areas have relatively recent histories of radical organizing by groups such as the Young Patriots. Today a handful of leftists have begun such an engagement, the most notable being the chapter organization Redneck Revolt, which attempts to compete with the militias on their own territory, even handing out anarcho-communist literature at gun shows.

47 In similar salmon-dependent forests such as the Great Bear Rainforest in British Columbia, some 80 percent of the forest's entire nitrogen supply comes from salmon. For more on the connection between salmon, nitrogen, and forest growth, see James M. Helfield and Robert J. Naiman, "Effects of Salmon-derived Nitrogen on Riparian Forest Growth and Implications for Stream Productivity," *Ecology*, LXXXII/9 (September 2001), pp. 2403–9.

3 The Iron City

1 For the city's early industrial development, see Matthew W. Klingle, *The Emerald City: An Environmental History of Seattle* (New Haven, CT, 2007).

2 For more on this process, see Deborah Cowen, *The Deadly Life of Logistics: Mapping Violence in Global Trade* (Minneapolis, MN, 2014).

3 A list of important events and some summary data have been compiled by the Washington State China Relations Council, available here: www.wscrc.org/WA-China.

4 The hubs are the Sodo-Georgetown-South Park stretch between the port of Seattle and Boeing field, the SeaTac-Tukwila-Kent complex sitting between the SeaTac airport and the Kent Valley Manufacturing Industrial Center, the Highway 167 freight corridor centered on the rail yards in Auburn and Algona, and the area in and around the Port of Tacoma.

5 The data here is employment shares and location quotients originally calculated from the Puget Sound Regional Council Covered Employment Estimates for 2013, summarized in my Master's Thesis: Phillip A. Neel, "Logistics Cities: Poverty, Immigration and Employment in Seattle's Southern Suburbs," University of Washington, Department of Geography (2015). Appendix B, Maps 1.1, 1.2, 1.5, 1.6, 1.14, and 1.15.

6   Jasper Bernes, "Logistics, Counterlogistics and the Communist Prospect," *Endnotes*, 3 (September 2013).

7   For more on the air freight industries in these cities in particular, see John Kasarda and Greg Lindsay, *Aerotropolis: The Way We'll Live Next* (New York, 2012).

8   Data from Ed Arnold, "The Largest Employers for Memphis in 2015," *Memphis Business Journal* (July 14, 2015).

9   Numbers obtained by author via the Census LODES database, processed using the Census on the Map area analysis summaries, available at http://onthemap.ces.census.gov.

10 "The New Map of Economic Growth and Recovery," *Economic Innovation Group* (May 2016), pp. 7–11.

11 Ibid., p. 17.

12 Ibid., pp. 21–3, figs 20–22.

13 For the data behind this, see the work of the University of Washington atmospheric scientist Cliff Mass, available at http://cliffmass.blogspot.com.

14 Data from the 2010–14 American Community Survey 5-year Data Profiles.

15 The exceptions to this trend is a handful of low-income tracts with high foreign-born population in the far north, near Everett, and a concentration of high-income tracts with high foreign-born population in the east-side tech suburbs around Bellevue, but these tracts remain low in overall diversity. All of this data, drawn from the 2010 Census, is available on the Mixed Metro project website: www. mixedmetro.us.

16 "The New Map of Economic Growth and Recovery," p. 15, fig. 15.

17 "Tracking the Low-wage Recovery: Industry, Employment and Wages," National Employment Law Project, www.nelp.org, April 27, 2014.

18 This is not assumed or intuited, but demonstrated in my Master's Thesis with origin-destination data from the Census LODES database, visible on Maps 4.1–4.4. The logistics clusters themselves are largely the same, though slightly offset due to the lack of residential properties in many of the industrial tracts. White Center, Tukwila, SeaTac, and Kent stand out as the major settlements, visible on Maps 2.0–2.21 and 3.1. See Neel, "Logistics Cities."

19 Alan Ehrenhalt, *The Great Inversion and the Future of the American City* (New York, 2012), p. 122.

20 Ibid., p. 121.

21 This trend is best visualized by a recent atlas of suburbia produced by the RCLCO Real Estate group, using categories drawn from the Urban Land Institute's most recent report on suburban housing. The atlas is available here: www.rclco.com/suburb-atlas. The report it accompanies is here: "Housing in the Evolving American Suburb," Urban Land Institute, www.uli.org, 2016.

22 Bernadette D. Proctor, Jessica L. Semega, and Melissa A. Kollar, "Income and Poverty in the United States: 2015," u.s. Census Bureau: Current Populaton Reports, September 2016.

23 For more data on the suburbanization of poverty, see the work of Elizabeth Kneebone and Alan Berube done on behalf of the Brookings Metropolitan Policy Institute, much of which is collected on their Confronting Suburban Poverty in America website: www.confrontingsuburbanpoverty.org.

24 "Ashland's Ore Docks, a Fascinating History," Wisconsin Central, www.wisconsincentral.net, 2010–16.

25 Roy L. Martin, "History of the Wisconsin Central," *Railroad and Locomotive Historical Society Bulletin*, 54 (January 1941), pp. 18–22.

26 There are notable exceptions to this, of which Chicago is the foremost, largely due to factors of size, physical geography, historical endowments, and its position at the center of several major logistics corridors.

27 See William H. Frey, *Diversity Explosion: How New Racial Demographics Are Remaking America* (Washington, DC, 2014).

28 Emily Badger, "Watch these Cities Segregate, even as they Diversify," CityLab, www.citylab.com, June 15, 2012.

29 Ehrenhalt, *The Great Inversion*, pp. 44–5.

30 Rebecca Solnit, "Detroit Arcadia," *Harper's*, www.harpers.org, July 2007.

31 Michael Snyder, "The Mayor of Detroit's Radical Plan to Bulldoze One Quarter of the City," *Business Insider*, www.businessinsider.com, March 10, 2010.

32 Ibid.

33 For an overview of the early years of this development, see George C. S. Lin, *Red Capitalism in South China: Growth and Development of the Pearl River Delta* (Vancouver, 2002).

34 For more on the middle-class demand for "special zones of eco-living," see Li Zhang, *In Search of Paradise: Middle-class Living in a Chinese Metropolis* (Ithaca, NY, 2010).

35 Lin, *Red Capitalism in South China*, p. 71.

36 Andy Sywak, "The South Rises Again! (In Automobile Manufacturing, That Is)," *New Geography*, www.newgeography.com, July 23, 2008.

37 These are all uneven dynamics, however, as certain Sunbelt states have been far less successful than others in terms of both job creation and migration. New Mexico and Mississippi have both lagged far behind their neighbors, and large swaths of Texas remain distant from the success of Austin, Dallas, or Houston. See Tim Henderson, "Americans Are Moving South, West Again," Pew Charitable Trusts, www.pewtrusts.org, January 8, 2016.

38 Eric Eidlin, "What Density Doesn't Tell Us about Sprawl," *Access Magazine*, 37 (Fall 2010).

39 Ehrenhalt, *The Great Inversion*, p. 170.

40 Robert J. Gordon, *The Rise and Fall of American Growth: The u.s. Standard of Living Since the Civil War* (Princeton, NJ, 2016), p. 104.

41 Ibid., pp. 166–7.

4 Oaths of Water

1 Oliver Milman, "Missouri Residents Pack Up and Leave as Once-rare Floods Become the New Normal," *The Guardian*, www.theguardian.com, January 8, 2016.

2 Ibid.

3 A convenience store and gas station common in the American Midwest and South. During the 2014 riots in Ferguson, Missouri, following the murder of unarmed black teenager Michael Brown, a QuikTrip that was alleged to have called the police on Brown was burned to the ground and subsequently became a gathering place for protestors.

4 This data comes from the u.s. Census and American Community Survey, all of which is reviewed here alongside a number of other sources: Phil A. Neel, "New Ghettoes Burning," *Ultra*, www.ultra-com.org, August 17, 2014.

5 Nathan Robinson, "The Shocking Finding from the DOJ's Ferguson Report that Nobody Has Noticed," *Huffington Post*, www.huffingtonpost.com, March 13, 2015.

6 Ibid.

7 Gwynn Guilford, "Ferguson—and Many Other American Cities—Wring Revenue from Black People and the Poor," *Quartz*, www.qz.com, August 28, 2014.

8 Ibid.

9 These trends are all detailed here: "Profiting from Probation: America's Offender-funded Probation Industry," Human Rights Watch, www.hrw.org, February 5, 2014.

10 Guilford, "Ferguson."

11 Sarah Parvini, "Anaheim Police Shooting Survivor Says Cops 'Shot Again and Again'," *Fox News Latino*, http://latino.foxnews.com, July 30, 2012.

12 "The Flatbush Rebellion," *Fire Next Time*, 2013, see https://eastcoastrenegades.wordpress.com.

13 Among the few remaining Maoist cults in the u.s., originating from one of the larger and more vibrant sects of the long-extinct "New Communist Movement," the RCP today is a shrinking, cloistered grouplet split between a mass of gray-haired baby boomers and a minority of young converts harvested from high schools in the inner city (particularly in places like New York and Chicago), rapidly indoctrinated in true Bible Belt fashion through exclusive reading lists

and total daily mobilization into the culture of the cult, which largely involves standing in front of other peoples' protests, finding brown people to hold up their signs (complete with URL and exclamation points) and screaming empty slogans toward the news cameras.

14 Paul Ekirch, *At Day's Close: Night in Times Past* (New York, 2006), p. 331.

15 See David Harvey, *Paris: Capital of Modernity* (New York, 2005).

16 Katie Sanders. "Ferguson, Mo. Has 50 White Police Officers, Three Black, NBC's Mitchell Claims," PunditFact, www.politifact.com, August 17, 2014.

17 Brian Mahoney, "Police Union Wants Protection Under Hate Crime Law," *Politico*, www.politico.com, January 5, 2015.

18 Jennifer Bain and Eileen A. J. Connelly, "Asian and Black Communities Square Off Over Cop Prosecution," *New York Post*, www.nypost.com, February 20, 2016.

19 See "The Flatbush Rebellion."

20 Key Macfarlane, "Riots of Passage," *Ultra*, www.ultra-com.org, May 12, 2015.

21 Ibid.

22 Ibid.

23 "What is Karst? And Why Is it Important?," The Karst Waters Institute (Leesburg, VA, 2016).

24 After the collapse of the New Communist Movement, many American radicals began a "long march through the institutions," joining progressive political campaigns, labor unions, NGOs, and city governments, ostensibly to begin to radicalize them from within. In many coastal cities, it is this crop of politicians who staff much of the current municipal power structure. It is possible that the influx of former Maoists into local government brought an element of protracted people's war to city management.

25 It should also be noted that it was very rare for such groups actually to overlap with the "working groups" formally established by the general assembly, even where "tactical" or "food" working groups had formed. Most working groups were at best nonfunctional and at worst obstructive to these advances.

26 David Kilcullen, *Out of the Mountains: The Coming Age of the Urban Guerrilla* (New York, 2015), p. 183.

27 Similar phenomena were visible in Ukraine, where football Ultras did play a role. For more detail on Hong Kong, see "Black Versus Yellow: Class Antagonism and Hong Kong's Umbrella Movement," *Ultra*, www.ultra-com.org, October 3, 2014.

28 Kilcullen, *Out of the Mountains*, pp. 181–2.

29 "Black Versus Yellow."

30 This is of necessity a brief review, and it elides the detail used by Clover in distinguishing previous eras of riot from our current era

of "riot prime." For his theory in its complete form, see Joshua Clover, *Riot. Strike. Riot* (New York, 2016).

31 Ibid., p. 157.

32 The claim is laid out most rigorously in his book: Andrew Kliman, *The Failure of Capitalist Production: Underlying Causes of the Great Recession* (London, 2011).

33 This is also not synonymous with a split between the managerial or supervisory strata of the working class and those beneath them, as Kliman makes clear in Andrew Kliman "More Misused Wage Data from 'Monthly Review': The Overaccumulation of a Surplus of Errors," *The Marxist Humanist Initiative*, April 10, 2013, available at www.marxisthumanistinitiative.org.

34 Andrew Kliman, "Are Corporations Really Hogging Workers' Wages?" Truthdig, www.truthdig.com, April 9, 2014.

35 The Invisible Committee, *To Our Friends* (Cambridge, MA, 2015), p. 81.

36 A suite of other charges, including murder, was initially leveled against Boosie, but he was ultimately exonerated by a jury of everything but the drug charges and several probation violations.

37 Laura Dimon, "A Modern Day Slave Plantation Exists and Is Thriving in the Heart of America," Mic, www.mic.com, May 8, 2014.

38 "Top 25 Water Ports by Weight: 2004 (Million Short Tons)," Freight Facts and Figures, 2006. Federal Highway Administration, November 2006.

39 Daniel Denvir, "Sunday's Police Riot in Baton Rouge: Anti-brutality Protests Met with Brutality," Salon, www.salon.com, July 15, 2016.

40 Michael Edison Hayden and David Caplan "Protests Continue in Baton Rouge and St. Paul Following Night of Arrests," ABC News, www.abcnews.go.com, July 20, 2016.

41 "'Open to Unorthodox Methods': An Interview on the Baton Rouge Uprising," Rigole Rise, http://rigolerise.wordpress.com, August 27, 2016.

42 Kilcullen, pp. 188–99.

43 "'Open to Unorthodox Methods'."

44 "Fortress L.A. in the 21st Century," Lucha No Feik, www.luchanofeik. club, August 24, 2016.

45 Ibid.

46 Frederic Jameson, *An American Utopia: Dual Power and the Universal Army* (New York, 2016), pp. 1–96.

Acknowledgments

In keeping with its politics, this book is essentially a collaborative text. It's narrated in the first person, but the ideas are wrought from collective experience, as all ideas are. It was written as much by the Hinterland as about it. In this regard, there are too many people in too many countries to thank for the stories repeated here. But a few individuals were essential to the process of drawing this into its present form. In the literal sense, this would not have been a book if Paul Mattick, editor of the Field Notes series, had not asked me to write it, or if Vivian Constantinopoulos, Editorial Director at Reaktion, had not facilitated its production. Meanwhile, the politics of the book could never have been articulated without the help of numerous discussions with friends across the world. Again, there are too many to thank in entirety. But the constellation of connections that emerged from the Occupy years was essential. In particular, Derek, Lainie, and Harper helped to anchor lofty political abstractions in the firm ground of class experience. At the same time, traveling and talking with Jasmine, Matt, Feifei, and Lala in southern China helped to provide a global perspective, and a series of small talks at Hong Kong Reader bookstore laid the skeleton for this book by challenging me to narrate the geography of class and conflict in America to an audience with very different presumptions. Altogether, then, the final product is both collective and global, as any good communist writing should be.